To India
With Love

To India With Love

The Biography of Carol Hastings

by
Darlene Saunders

Published by Redeemer Books
P.O. Box 15
Winamac, Indiana, USA

To India With Love

ISBN 1-877607-54-1

Published by Redeemer Books
P.O. Box 15
Winamac, Indiana, USA

Library of Congress Cataloging-in-Publication Data

Saunders, Darlene.
  To India with love : the biography of Carol Hastings / by Darlene Saunders.
    p. cm.
  ISBN 1-877607-54-1
  1. Hastings, Carol. 2. Missionaries, Medical--India--Biography.
3. Nurses--India--Biography. I. Title.
R722.32.H38S28   1992
610.69 ' 5 ' 092--dc20
[B]   92-36967

To the members and friends at the Vallejo Bible Church, for their faithful prayers and support over the years. "According to the power of God, Who hath saved us, and called us with an holy calling, not according to our works but according to his own purpose and grace, which was given us in Christ Jesus before the world began." II Timothy 1:8b-9

Carol Hastings

Carol Hastings

ENDORSEMENTS

If you are wanting to read the exploits of a well publicized, 20th Century missionary, you have picked up the wrong book. On the other hand, if you want to be encouraged by God's ministry to and through one of His humble servants, then read on.

God's care of and blessings through Carol Hastings during thirty-eight years of strenuous nursing and village evangelism, in the dark and idolatrous land of India, says much about the faithfulness of Him who ever lives to make intercession for us.

Those thirty-eight years also give clear testimony to the commitment, the courage, the compassion, and the Christ likeness of the subject of this biographical sketch. More than once her life was threatened by Satan inspired Hindu mobs.

But Carol Hastings has been faithful and you will most certainly meet men and women from India in Heaven because God has honored her ministry. Keep on reading. You'll be glad you did.

Don Hillis, TEAM

Finally, a book about one of our finest missionaries. My wife and I have known this sincere and deeply committed missionary to India since her entrance in nursing school. We have seen her personal conversion to Christ, her steady growth in grace, her first concern for India, and her total abandonment to the will of God wherever it led. In fact, Carol has been a missionary from the time of her conversion, fully involved in praying, giving and telling others the Good News.

This book about Carol Joy Hastings' life and work will give its reader insight into the daily struggles of the missionary as well as a deeper appreciation for the work of the Lord Himself in the harvest fields.

India and other fields need more career servants of Christ like Carol Hastings.

Roger Andrus, first president of Calvary Bible Coll., Kansas City, MO

Called by God to serve in India, Carol Hastings responded by faith, and was sent to that land by her home church. Her experiences as a missionary nurse bring us face to face with the reaction of Indian people to the gospel. Sometimes there is outright rejection, sometimes there is the faint recognition of the truth. Each chapter of this book points to a loving God who has the power to protect His servants and to save those who walk in spiritual darkness. This is a book that lifts up the Lord Jesus, and I hope you will enjoy reading it.

Richard M. Winchell, General Director, TEAM

CONTENTS

FOREWORD

You may never see her name on the same page of missionary history with Carey, Livingstone, Taylor, Slessor, or Carmichael. But I am persuaded that the name of Carol Hastings will figure prominently in God's final accounting of world mission activity. Why? Take a couple of hours to read this book and find out.

You'll discover that above all, Carol was obedient to "the heavenly vision" received from the Lord of the Harvest. Nothing could deter her from following Christ to India—not even a broken engagement on the day before her wedding. No one could keep her from sharing her love for Christ. She witnessed of her Savior to one and all, including patients, travelers, friends, strangers, and family. God calls her "wise" because she has won many of these people to faith in Christ.

Carol understood and applied the Scriptures in life situations. On one occasion the enemy tried to destroy Carol through discouragement. The mission doctor had diagnosed her as having leprosy. Her tears of fear and disappointment initially were soon replaced by meditation on Joshua 1:9 and Isaiah 41:10 and 13, passages she had committed to memory many years earlier. Characteristically, Carol's understanding of God through his Word held her steady during this difficult trial.

I have a special interest in this story. God used Carol Hastings to help direct me to missionary service in Bolivia. I was eight years of age and a new Christian when Carol first came to our home as a guest. She visited us often, both before going to India in 1945 and on subsequent furloughs. I saw the beauty of Jesus in her. She had a warm smile and an infectious laugh. Carol was a hard worker, too. I could hardly believe my eyes that day on our California farm when she plucked twenty chickens for the Mission Springs family camp. And to Carol, I was not just an insignificant little boy who was to be seen and not heard. She took time to explain the Scriptures to me and urged me to commit my life to Christ.

God has always delighted in demonstrating His truth through flesh and blood people. In Carol Hastings He found the willing channel to do just that.

Ron Wiebe
Deputy General Director
SIM International

ACKNOWLEDGEMENTS

I am deeply grateful to the following people who helped make this book what it is: first and foremost, Carol, who graciously cooperated with me over the "long haul" so that the story of how God used her in India could be told; the editors at Redeemer Books, particularly Marshall Nelson; Chuck Miles, who designed the cover; Ron Wiebe, Deputy General Director of SIM International, who wrote the foreword; Don Hillis of TEAM, who wrote the introduction; Richard Winchell (General Director of TEAM), Roger Andrus (past president of Calvary Bible College, whose wife led Carol to the Lord), and Harold Freeman (past National Executive Director of the Independent Fundamental Churches of America), who encouraged me and wrote their endorsements. My husband Larry has been of particular blessing in reading and listening, as well as putting up with late meals and all the inconveniences of a writing wife. Besides these, God has given me a multitude of friends, family, and coworkers who knew of this work and encouraged me along the way. I thank God for each one of you.

Darlene

INTRODUCTION

High on the list of recommended reading for Christians is the biography of God's servants. Just such a book is this story of Carol Hastings, missionary to India, where she invested thirty-eight years of her life seeking to reach those in need of the knowledge of our Lord Jesus Christ.

How do missionaries receive their start into this kind of a career? The whole world is needy; where should they go? What preparations are expected, and how do they go about getting ready? It takes money to reach a foreign field and live there while they serve the Lord with the skills acquired and share the message of saving grace; how is it realized? What is it like to go to a strange country, and what are the inner feelings of the missionary who undertakes this kind of service? All these things and more are provided in this record of Carol's life from a farm family at the age of twelve, through nurse's training, Bible Institute, establishing a church home in Vallejo, California, deputation work after choosing a missionary agency, the trip to Egypt and Bombay, and finally to Amalner, India in 1943.

Health problems are faced, beginning with amoebic dysentery in Egypt and anguish of facing suspected leprosy in a country where this disease is common.

Persecutions by hostile villages during efforts to bring the gospel to people ensnared in idolatry demonstrate the care of our God for His servants through times of stress. Perplexities on the part of the missionary over how to share personal problems and the importance of prayer support are faithfully given.

Many tests in the perfecting of this missionary's faith revealed to her opportunities to witness in our Lord's strength to the saving and keeping power of Jesus Christ.

Accounts of difficult spiritual and physical problems faced by this missionary nurse make it difficult to lay this book down.

This reviewer of the manuscript counted it a privilege to be able to read Carol's story of her life, having personally known her and many of the people who had influence in her life over the years. It was my privilege to have pastored the Vallejo Bible Church that undertook her support in those early beginnings of this fascinating account of her life. It is highly recommended to take a place on your bookshelf.

Dr. Harold Freeman

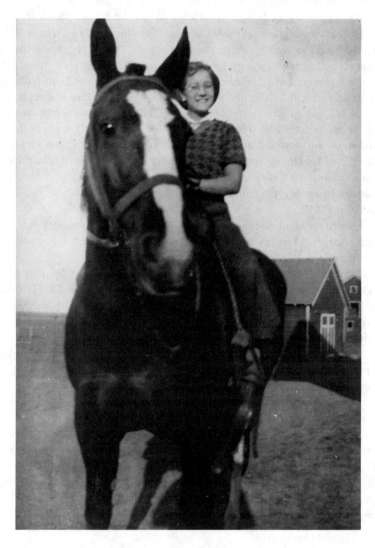

On the farm in Pierpont, South Dakota

Chapter 1

NEW LIFE IN CHRIST

Life at home, the way Carol remembered it, was just a memory. The little farm outside of Pierpont, North Dakota, might look the same, but families change. Every year the family at home would grow smaller as the Hastings children, one by one, finished high school and struck out on their own. Her trips home would be only for vacations.

She'd thought this through many times in the year between high school graduation and beginning nurses training. In the boarding house at Pierpont High School she enjoyed sharing a room with her sister. Muriel's encouragement helped her through the difficult senior year, including editing the yearbook and representing her class as valedictorian. Now she faced Minneapolis and Eitel Hospital alone.

"No, more time for reflecting on the past," she told herself. She set her suitcase down in the middle of the single room. This was her assigned room at the home for nursing students. The echo of her voice startled her. "If this is to be my new home I'll need to fill it up with a few personal things," she whispered.

Picking up her class schedule, she welcomed its fullness. There would be no time to feel sorry for herself at Eitel Hospital in Minneapolis. With a sigh she opened the top bureau drawer, then turned to place her suitcase on the single bed and unclasp its lock. She had no friends from home here as there had been at Pierpont High, and after the experience of being considered a country hick in high school, she approached friend-making cautiously. She knew only one person in Minneapolis, her uncle, Dr. DeForest. She thought of him with pride, for he was an instructor here at Eitel. A smile brightened her face. Maybe eventually she could enroll in one of his classes. She hoped to see him from time to time on the campus.

After studying a map of the hospital and classrooms, Carol had no trouble finding her way to the classes the next day. At lunchtime she became confused but soon realized she only needed to follow the direction other students were walking to get to the cafeteria. Food scents triggering hunger pains told her she had chosen the right way. She rounded a corner to find the lunch line extending into the hall.

"If I only had a place to put these books down, I could manage the tray better," she said aloud to no one in particular.

A girl behind her said, "I think there are some shelves just inside the door."

Carol turned to say thank you and instantly recognized her. "Don't we have some classes together? I'm Carol."

"Yes. We've been together most of the morning. I'm Mary. I sit two seats behind you in first period."

After choosing their food they ate together, discussing many of the same career dreams.

Over lunch, Mary and Carol discovered they roomed on the same floor. The next day they began walking to and from their classes together. Carol appreciated Mary's calm, quiet manner and mature attitude. When Carol could not understand the behavior of some of the students, she shared her worries with Mary.

One morning, early in the semester, Carol stepped out of her room into a hallway buzzing with gossip.

"What is all the fuss?" Carol asked as she caught up with Mary.

"One of the first year students is in trouble for coming in an hour late last night," Mary explained.

"The same girl who did that last week?" Carol asked.

Mary nodded. "So now she is on probation."

"I don't understand," Carol said, stepping quickly to keep up with Mary's long stride. "I want to have a good time while I'm here at Eitel too."

Mary slowed a bit. "There's nothing wrong with good fun on our free time," she agreed.

Carol went on. "But I am confused. Some of the students seem to go bad once they've left their homes. They couldn't have learned those ways at home."

Mary shrugged and strode off ahead of Carol again. "I'm sure you're right. You'd think even unchristian homes would at least teach moral values," she said.

Carol checked her watch. As usual they would get to class just in time. She didn't quite understand what Mary meant by her statement about unchristian homes, but she continued.

"Nurses should know better than to do things that will hurt their bodies. It scares me. I wonder if it will happen to me too. I don't want to be like them," she puffed.

They hurried through the classroom door and found their desks. "It pays to live close to the Lord," Mary said.

Carol paused. She didn't know what Mary meant by that statement. Her thoughts were interrupted by the instructor asking for her homework. "No time to worry about Mary's statement now," she decided, taking out her book. Sometimes Mary left her puzzled but Carol did not like to show her ignorance by asking her to explain.

Carol had new things to consider as well as difficult subjects to learn in the nursing program. There was no time to think things through to logical conclusions.

At the end of the first quarter students received assignments to the university hospital for pediatrics and psychology training. Carol and Mary met for lunch the day room assignments were given.

"Are we on the same floor again?" Carol asked, peeking over her food tray to see if Mary's assignment slip was visible.

"Just a minute, nosy," Mary laughed. She set down her tray. "I'm on...."

"Hey, is that my slip?" Carol interrupted.

"No."

Carol took out her slip and handed it to Mary.

"They're the same. We're roommates, Carol!"

The room assignment delighted both girls. Carol knew she would have opportunity to glean from Mary's knowledge. The day they moved to the university campus Carol again brought up her fears about "going bad."

As Mary unpacked her books, the title of one caught her eye.

"This book helped me," Mary said, holding it out to Carol. "Maybe it would help you too."

Carol took the book from her hands.

"The Virtuous Woman by Lowry," she read. "I'm not sure that fits, but I'll read it," she promised, and as soon as she finished organizing her half of the room she began to read.

A few days later Carol returned the book to Mary.

"How did you like it?" Mary asked, carefully placing it in the space she had left for it on her shelves.

"It's okay, but I don't believe all that stuff," Carol said. "For one thing, I don't see what could be so bad about going to movies. Movies are just stories. You read books. Movies are just stories like books. The same with dancing. We went to a lot of dances back on the farm. It's like playing a game, just jumping around."

Mary quietly sat down at her desk and turned to face Carol. "But don't you see things in movies you wouldn't do yourself?" she asked.

"Sure, just like in books," Carol defended.

"Would you go with a date into a tavern?" Mary persisted.

"Of course not," Carol answered.

"But in the movie your mind goes wherever the movie takes you. In effect you've been in a tavern if you've been to a movie with a scene in a tavern."

Mary turned back to her studies.

"That's silly. It's just a story," Carol argued, turning to her own books. But she wasn't convinced Mary was wrong.

The next time Carol came home from a movie she found Mary studying for a test.

"How was the movie?" Mary asked, stifling a yawn.

Carol didn't know how to answer. It had been a good movie. There were parts she knew Mary would not have enjoyed, parts that now bothered Carol.

"Oh, it was good—a good story," she replied. Mary said no more. Carol had the feeling Mary had been praying for her throughout the evening. As usual, Mary's Bible lay close by her pile of school books.

A few days later Carol had a movie date with a young man she had not dated before. Mary watched her carefully prepare for the evening, admiring her outfit and the new white gloves Carol had bought for the occasion. Carol welcomed the social evening, away from her studies.

But from the moment he picked her up in his roadster, Carol had the feeling that this was not going to be a memorable evening. Her gentleman friend seemed ill at ease. After helping Carol into the car he went around to the driver's side and settled himself.

"Nice evening," he mumbled.

"Yes, it's neither too cold nor too hot," Carol agreed.

The young man started the car and gave his full attention to driving.

After several moments of silence, Carol thought, this is ridiculous. She tried to think of something to say but only nursing subjects came to mind.

"It's good to get away from studying pediatrics," she finally said.

"Huh? Oh, yeh. We're learning logarithms now," he answered.

Carol didn't know anything about logarithms, not even enough to ask an intelligent question. Silence continued until she tried another subject.

"We're studying psychology in the morning classes."

She intended to ask if he had studied any psychology but he interrupted.

"Next week we start field work on a construction site."

They pulled into a parking place so they stopped attempting to converse.

Inside the theater Carol's date led her to seats near the back row. Shortly after the film credits began, he asked, "Can you see well from here?"

Carol hesitated before answering, "I can see fine, can't you?"

"Let's find a better seat," he said. He got up and led Carol to seats in the second row. The movie began and Carol concentrated on the story. She rubbed her neck and her date said, "These seats are too close for you, aren't they?"

Carol started to protest, but he was already excusing himself as he crawled over the people sitting between them and the aisle. She had no recourse but to follow him to new seats in the center of the auditorium.

Finally settled, Carol relaxed but soon she was telling herself, "This is a boring movie." She shifted her body in the theater seat. "Nothing is happening, not even in scenes that would shock Mary. I'll be glad when it is over."

She glanced over to see if her date seemed as bored as she but he stared intently at the screen.

"How can he be so interested in this boring story?" Carol wondered.

Finally the movie ended. The lights came on then they made their way to the car.

"Now maybe we'll do something fun," Carol hoped, as he helped her into the car. It was a warm evening. She hoped they would stop at a soda fountain. He started the car and gave all his attention to driving. Carol smoothed her dress, then looked down and noticed her bare hands. Where were her new gloves?

She looked in her purse but they were not there. Her date looked over to see what she was searching for.

"My gloves," she explained. "I must have left them at the theater."

The young man barely took his attention from the road.

"I don't remember any gloves," he said. "What color were they?"

"White, of course," Carol snapped. "I had them on when we went into the theater."

"Well, we moved two times in there. There's no telling where you dropped them. Besides, the theater building's closed by now. No point in going back to look."

"He could at least act like he cares," Carol thought. She did not trust herself to say any more and her date made no offer to stop at a soda fountain. By the time they arrived at the dorm Carol was too angry to speak to him at all: angry with him, angry about her gloves, angry she had even gone to a movie, and angry with Mary.

She thought, "I wish Mary would stop praying for me. I can't have any fun any more."

As she watched her date drive away, she said to herself, "No more movies. I'll just be content to go to the dances. They're more fun anyway." She did not tell Mary about her disastrous evening.

In a few days Carol had her opportunity to enjoy a dance at the university. This time she organized a group of student nurses and they went together. In high school she and her girl friends had gone to dances together and had a wonderful time so Carol looked forward to the evening with excitement. It would be a good break from the hard studies. She even tried to get Mary to join them, but Mary chose to stay alone at the dorm. Carol hoped Mary wouldn't spend the whole evening praying for her.

Carol was not surprised no one asked her to dance at first but she expected she would soon make friends and dance the night away. She busied herself about the refreshment table, striking up a conversation with anyone coming to the punch bowl. The boys were friendly, but each one was already occupied with another young lady or ready to sit out a dance or two and rest.

"I didn't have any fun at all," Carol complained to the other nurses on the way home. They all agreed it had not been nearly as much fun as they had expected.

"At least it was a break from our books," one girl said.

Carol nodded. She didn't tell them her suspicion of the reason for her disappointing evening: Mary must have been praying she wouldn't have a good time, and that no one would ask her to dance. She was angry again, with Mary and with the fellows because they hadn't asked her to dance. Again she decided not to mention the evening to Mary.

Every day she wondered about Mary's praying and reading her Bible so faithfully.

"Does she think she's better than I am because she reads the Bible and prays? I'm as good a person as she is. I don't do a lot of bad things. I don't swear. I give up things."

One day Mary asked Carol to go with her to a week of special church meetings.

"Here's my chance to show her I'm just as good as she is," Carol thought as she agreed to go with her.

After work the next evening they almost ran the 15 blocks to the church. They arrived so late that all seats were filled except those in the second row. Just as the girls sat down, Dr. Walter Wilson, the special speaker, asked, "How many of you brought your Bibles?"

Four young men sitting in the front row waved their Bibles. Carol couldn't believe it. Young men excited about the Bible! She decided to pay close attention to the message. "I thought only the old, homely, or crippled were fanatically religious. I wonder what these young men find so exciting about the Bible."

Dr. Wilson spoke about being saved, and going either to heaven or to hell. Carol had not heard about being saved before, but she thought, "I don't understand but I do want to be sure I'm going to heaven."

Dr. Wilson gave an example from his own life. He was not only a preacher, but a medical doctor. He also owned a clothing factory. One young girl who operated a sewing machine in his factory was under conviction of sin. She wanted to talk to Dr. Wilson. She ran a sewing machine needle through her finger so she would have an excuse to go to his office, in the hope that he would tell her how to be saved. He bound up her finger and told her to be more careful, but he did not say anything about the Lord.

She did this three times. The last time he told her she was too careless and would have to find another job. She began to cry, and told him, "I did it on purpose. I wanted you to tell me how to get rid of my sin."

The doctor was ashamed he had not talked to her about the Lord. He showed her the way of salvation, and she was saved.

Carol wondered, "What does being saved mean?"

After the meeting, Isobel, another student nurse, walked home with them. Carol remained deep in thought, while the other two girls talked about the meeting.

Mary asked, "Isobel, are you saved?"

Isobel answered, "Yes, I am."

"Why doesn't she ask me?" Carol wondered. "If she'd ask maybe she could tell me how to be saved. I know that's what I need to do."

Because Mary read her Bible and prayed, Carol reasoned that must be the way to be saved. She didn't know how to pray and she didn't understand what she read, but she kept trying.

After the week of Dr. Wilson's meetings, Carol and Mary attended other meetings. One evening they went to a special evangelistic rally where the pastor spoke from Romans 12:1 and 2. The Holy Spirit really convicted Carol about giving her life to the Lord, but she didn't know how to do it. She was still trying to understand how to be saved. She began to feel she wanted the Lord to have her whole life.

At the end of the message Mary went forward to dedicate her life to the Lord. Carol followed her, intending to give her life to serve Him too. A woman named Evelyn talked with her.

"Why did you come forward tonight?" Evelyn asked.

Carol smiled. "I want to give my life to the Lord."

"Wonderful! When did you first become interested in the Lord?"

"At the Walter Wilson meetings," Carol answered.

"Then you've already received Jesus as your Savior. You just need to be baptized," Evelyn declared. "Would you be interested in coming to our new convert classes?"

"I guess so," Carol answered. "Is that what I need to do?"

"Every Christian needs to follow the Lord in the waters of baptism."

So Carol agreed to attend the classes, hoping they would explain how to be saved.

Back in her room at the nurses home she groaned, "How do you get saved? I've tried and tried but I'm not getting saved!"

A few days later, Helen, the maid at the nurses home, received the Lord at a meeting, and she shared her experience with Mary. The next day, at lunch in the dining hall, Mary asked, "Did you hear that Helen got saved last night?"

Carol answered, "Oh, no! How did she get saved?"

Mary answered, "Helen went to a meeting and she went forward."

Carol thought, "Well, I did that too. And I didn't get saved." She stared into her soup. Nothing made sense.

But Mary went on. "The pastor talked to her and told her about the Lord dying for her sins, and that He rose again. He said, 'Just let the Lord save you and He will save you.'"

Carol thought, "If Helen can get saved that way, I can too."

Later that evening Carol confided in Mary, "I'm finally saved. I believe God wants to save me and that He will save me, so I let Him save me. And I got saved right there in the dining hall this afternoon."

Mary hugged her and cried. She had been praying a long time for her roommate. God finally answered.

Chapter 2

SHARING THE GOOD NEWS

"Work out your own salvation with fear and trembling!" Carol's uncle, Dr. DeForest, tossed the Scripture verse back in answer to her witness. She had quoted Ephesians 2:8-9: "By grace are ye saved through faith."

Since her graduation from nurses training, she did not know where the Lord would lead her and she had wanted to share her faith with her uncle. However, his retort surprised her. She had no answer and her confusion and shame sent her running to her friend and confidante, Mary.

"I don't understand what's happening," she complained. "When I used those same verses to witness to my brother, God saved him."

Mary reminded her, "Yes, but not right away. It took almost nine months, remember?"

"Well, I just don't understand. Being saved is the most important thing in life—in all eternity. Everyone should want to receive Jesus."

"Those of us who know Him, we know the joy of the Christian life," Mary agreed. "But remember, you didn't come to the Lord the first time you heard about Him either."

Carol laughed. "No, I didn't recognize the truth, and I didn't understand a lot of what I heard. Even after I realized the Lord called me to Christian service I didn't understand how to receive Him as my own Savior first."

The girls quickly changed from their uniforms to go to a missionary conference at the church. "Speaking of serving the Lord, aren't you enjoying all these missionary speakers this week?" Mary asked.

Carol reached for her hair brush. "Yes, it's almost too much," she agreed. "Every time a missionary speaks I think, 'That's the place I want to be a missionary. I want to go.' If he's from China, I want to go to China. Africa? I'll go to Africa; or India; or wherever the speaker came from."

Mary slipped into her shoes and strode to the door. "Yes, you're like me. We see the whole world's need."

Mary had been dating a young man named Roger Andrus but right after Mary graduated, Roger went to Phoenix to earn money so he could attend a Bible school in Minneapolis. Mary eagerly looked for his frequent letters and often shared parts of them with Carol. Carol watched how Mary and Roger determined what the Lord wanted them to do with their lives. As a new Christian, many times she found it hard to decide what she should do. It helped to be able to learn from experienced Christians.

One hot summer afternoon, Carol came home to find Mary excitedly waving another letter from Roger. She barely had a chance to sit down before Mary began telling her about a school in Phoenix.

"Listen to this," Mary said. She began reading, "There's a Bible institute right here in Phoenix. The Lord led me right to it as I walked home a different way the other afternoon. It's not very big, but I've talked with the president, Mr. Bancroft. He sounds like the Bible teacher I would like to learn from."

Mary raised her eyes to see Carol's response.

"Sounds good," Carol said. "What else does he say?"

"Well, he wants me to pray about it with him, but I think he's already made up his mind to go there for his Bible training."

"But I thought you two had decided he would go to Minneapolis so he would be closer. It's been hard enough on you to have him gone this summer."

"It sure has," Mary agreed. But she was quick to add, "Of course, we want the Lord's will. This is an important decision."

Carol had never seen her look so despondent.

"Couldn't you go with him to Phoenix? I'm sure there are hospitals needing nurses in that city too."

"Pray about it with us," Mary answered, and Carol noticed a gleam return to her eye.

Roger's next letter confirmed Mary's guess, he had decided to enroll at PBI. Mary didn't read Carol her answers to Roger's letters, so she could only guess what their plans were, but a couple of weeks later Carol came home to an ecstatic Mary.

"We're getting married," she squealed, hugging her.

Carol hugged her back, setting aside her own fears of losing her roommate and friend.

"When is the wedding?" she asked.

"Next weekend. School starts in two weeks," Mary answered.

"We'd better get started," Carol laughed. She looked at Mary and added, "I'm so happy for you, but I'll really miss you. I envy Roger getting to go to a Bible institute where he can learn better ways to serve the Lord."

Mary sat down across from Carol and took her hands in hers.

"It will be wonderful. Carol, you should go too. What do you think?"

Carol shook her head. "It sounds too good to be true," she said. "How can I know what the Lord wants me to do?"

Mary added, "You've been saying you need training if you are going to be a missionary."

"Well, I don't know how to tell what God wants me to do. But I'm sure He wants me to get some more training before I become a missionary. Just talking to my uncle showed me that. I'll do this. If God doesn't make me sick or something before it's time to go, I'll go with you to Phoenix and enroll in the Bible institute. Are you sure you and Roger want me to come along?"

"Of course we do," Mary laughed. "Oh, this is the greatest. I get my new husband and my old roommate. We all get to go learn to serve the Lord together."

That settled, Carol and Mary spent the rest of the evening and the next few days getting ready for the wedding. Carol wrote to the Bible institute in Phoenix, telling them of her plans. They wrote back a letter of acceptance. It seemed like a whirlwind placed them at the end of summer in Phoenix, ready for a new kind of schooling and starting a new job at Good Samaritan Hospital.

Every student at Phoenix Bible Institute had a Christian service assignment. Carol's was to witness to patients at the hospital.

One evening, not long after Carol had settled into her new job, an old man was rushed to the emergency room with a heart attack. It was almost time for Carol to go off duty, but her first response was to pray for him. He was in critical condition. As she worked over him she prayed he might live, that she would be able to give him the Gospel, and that he would have the opportunity to be saved. She put him on oxygen and started him on intravenous medicines before she went home.

The next day she was relieved to find him still alive and beginning a slow recovery. From then on she witnessed to Frank every day and gave him tracts to read.

One day he objected. "I don't believe the Bible. I have been deep sea diving in the Red Sea and haven't found any chariot wheels; I've walked where Lot lived and I haven't seen a pillar of salt that looked like Lot's wife. So I don't believe the Bible."

Carol continued to pray for Frank. One evening, while working at her hospital desk, she heard the pattering of bare feet in the hall, then the sound of a body falling. She ran to find Frank lying on the floor. She quickly called his doctor and they put him back to bed. After the doctor left, she asked Frank, "Why did you get up?"

He answered, "I was scared. I thought I was going to go to hell right now. I saw a vision over in the corner—two buddies that used to dive with me. They came up out of the water, all dripping, and they called, 'Come on, Frank. It's time for you.'

"I was afraid I was dying—right then—because they are already dead. So I wanted to come out and ask you again how to be saved."

Carol explained the way of salvation to him again. Later, alone in his room, he reread a tract she had given him, then signed it, acknowledging his trust in the Lord Jesus Christ. The next day, when Carol came to work, the other nurses told her, "We don't know what's happened to Mr. Crawley. He's really different today." Right away Carol knew her prayers had been answered.

Immediately Frank's life completely changed. Where before his habit was to curse everything, his favorite expression became "Praise the Lord!"

A few days later Frank asked Carol to find a poor person to give his old World War I military coat to. She thought, "Frank, you're the one who needs it. You're poor," but a generous spirit had replaced his former greedy ways.

The Lord gave Carol other opportunities to witness for Him. She worked in the county ward, taking care of patients who could not afford to pay for medical services. One day the ambulance brought in a young Mexican girl who had gone through an abortion and developed an infection with a high fever. Carol bathed her and began to talk to her about the Lord. Maria did not respond right away but Carol faithfully talked to her every day, as she had with Frank. One day Maria accepted Christ as her Savior too.

Because her physical condition did not improve, Maria was put into a private room. No one visited her so Carol spent as much time with her as possible, both on duty and off. One night Carol stopped at the Andruses' to tell them of Maria's final moments.

"When she died she raised her hands into the air and had a glowing smile. It seemed like she was being received by the angels in heaven," she reported.

Though saddened at Maria's death, Mary and Roger rejoiced with Carol that another sinner they had been praying for had found the Savior in time.

Chapter 3

A SERVANT'S CALLING

"God is saving many in India, because many babies are taken to be with the Lord before they grow up."

The missionary conference speaker's words hammered in Carol's mind. She hurried to the prayer meeting, impelled by the urgency of India's need.

Dropping to her knees by a folding chair, she barely waited for a break in the prayer time. "Please, Lord. You've laid this burden on my heart. Is this where you want me to serve you? Show me Your will," she begged.

In the silence as she paused to think about her life's work, God answered by putting a memorized verse in her mind, "Also I heard the voice of the Lord, saying, Whom shall I send, and who will go for us? Then said I, Here am I, send me."

Like Isaiah, Carol yielded to God's will, "Here am I. Send me."

Carol took her questions about decisions and perplexing theology to her pastor/instructor, Richard Foster. Now she eagerly sought him out to share the burden God placed on her heart.

She found him strolling with another student. Waiting for her opportunity, she followed along just outside of hearing. At the men's dorms the young man turned off the main walkway and Carol quickened her pace before Mr. Foster's stride carried him too far ahead.

"Well, I can see something's happening in your life," he announced, waiting for her to catch up.

Carol needed no prompting to relate to him how the Lord seemed to be directing her to India.

"Do you think that means God is calling me to go to India? I don't know how He calls anybody," she concluded.

Carol would long remember Pastor Foster's wise counsel: "I think you should believe the Lord has called you. You should keep praying and keep working to that end; and if He keeps leading you that way, you will be assured of God's will; but if you feel, as time goes on, that your heart is not led that way, then you will see that perhaps it was just an emotional experience."

As they parted at the dining hall, Carol determined to follow his advice. Throughout the following weeks she continued praying and talking to others about being a missionary and the Lord kept giving assurance that it was His will for her to go to India.

Carol had enjoyed nurses training, but she thrilled at the opportunity to study the Bible. Every class left her with many questions answered and many more unanswered.

"Carol, you have so many questions," her roommate Edith said one afternoon. They hurried to the library to gather report material.

"Oh, I know. I did it again," Carol moaned. "It's a wonder they let me back in the classes."

Edith led the way up the steps. "The teachers don't get upset by your interruptions," she soothed. "And sometimes it leads to lively discussions."

Carol paused at the library door. "But it may not be what the instructors had planned to discuss that class period," she worried.

"Then they should be thankful for someone like you to speak up and ask for explanations. At least then they know they're teaching something that isn't already understood by everyone."

Some students at the library tables looked up as they came in, so Carol squelched her answer, but she wondered just how thankful she would be for someone who always seemed to interrupt the lecture. She'd have to listen more carefully to see if she couldn't learn to understand more Bible truths on her own instead of taking class time.

Edith helped Carol understand many things, particularly practical aspects of the Christian life. One night Carol came home from work to find Edith still awake, sitting on her bed and looking sick.

"What's the matter with you?" Carol asked, dropping her purse and sitting down beside her.

The dark circles under Edith's eyes deepened and she appeared even more pale as she answered.

"I've stolen some ink," Edith confided.

Carol couldn't imagine Edith stealing anything. She looked into her eyes to understand how serious Edith felt.

"What did you do?" Carol asked.

"I filled my pen down in the library without asking," she said, near tears.

Such a trivial thing, Carol might have laughed, but she understood how important this was to Edith. Her conscience had not allowed her to sleep. She thought, "I might have taken it and never even felt convicted about it. I've got to have a tender conscience like Edith has."

They knelt to pray together. Edith confessed her sin and promised to make it right in the library tomorrow. Carol asked for a tender conscience so there would be nothing in her life to displease the Lord.

Carol and Edith spent many hours fellowshiping together, often with two young men, Beam and Warren. As the newest "babe in Christ", Carol reveled in the opportunity to learn all about the Christian life, in the classroom and out of it. Her friends encouraged her. She particularly thanked the Lord for Warren's testimony.

Frequently Carol found Warren waiting for her at the library where they studied together, or saving her a place in the dining hall where they lingered after the meal to review Bible memory verses together. Whenever Carol's work schedule permitted her to attend a social event, Warren would be her date. They didn't talk much about their feelings for each other but Carol felt Warren was "interested" in her.

It was natural to share her feelings about the missionary conference with Warren.

"You know, I think the Lord has called me to India," Carol said, pulling a missionary tract out of her Bible. They were enjoying the shady area outside the dining hall before Carol had to get ready for work.

"You remember that India is the place the Lord is directing me, don't you?" Warren asked. He reached over to see which tract she had.

"You said you wanted to be a missionary, but I don't remember hearing about how you came to that idea," Carol answered.

"It was while I attended the BIOLA Conference," he explained. "Very much like the way the Lord has spoken to you: the Lord impressed my heart with the need of Indians to hear the Gospel."

His urgency thrilled Carol. How exciting it would be to serve the Lord in India with this intense young man.

Controlling her voice, Carol answered, "I want to do what the Lord wants, and India sounds like such a needy place. I hope it's not just the glamour of going to a strange, foreign country. I hope it isn't just an emotional experience, like Mr. Foster mentioned."

"We can pray about it together," Warren suggested. "Even after this semester when I'm at Westmont, I'll still pray about God's leading you."

Carol didn't like to think about his going to another Bible school, but his promise comforted her.

Summer vacation followed right on the heels of the missionary conference, giving some relief from the heavy schedule of classes. Many students who worked in the Phoenix area, including Carol and Edith, continued to live at the Bible institute during the summer. One Saturday morning Edith awakened Carol by announcing, "Carol, I've been keeping a secret from you for several weeks now. I'm just going to burst if I don't tell someone."

Carol had come in around midnight from working at the hospital and she enjoyed sleeping a little later on Saturdays, catching up on the rest she missed during the work week. But Edith fairly glowed with excitement, so Carol sat up and rubbed her eyes, trying to appear attentive. Carol guessed that the secret might have to do with Edith's relationship to Beam Shaeffer, her steady boyfriend.

"Well, what is it?" Carol asked.

"Beam and I are getting married this evening," Edith announced.

"This evening?" Carol cried. "Why, that doesn't even give me time... why, I can't even get off work to be there!" she sputtered.

"I know. We wanted to keep it a secret, so we couldn't invite many guests," she explained, pacing from her desk to Carol's bed.

Carol swung her feet over the side of the bed.

"What will the school say?" she wondered. "Oh, I'm so happy for you. I know you and Beam were made for each other, but there's going to be a stir."

"Now don't try to talk me out of it," Edith laughed. "We've had this planned for a long while. It's been hard enough to keep it secret."

"I'm sure it has," Carol nodded, "especially from your own roommate."

"I do hope you won't be angry about it," Edith said, opening her closet. She took out her largest suitcase and put it on her bed.

"Here I go, losing another roommate... and for the same reason," Carol said. "No, I'm not angry. Just disappointed I can't be there to see it happen."

She did what she could to help Edith decide what to take for her short, week-end honeymoon. By the time Beam picked her up in the early afternoon, they had agreed Edith could get the rest of her belongings the next week. Carol promised not to tell anyone until Beam and Edith made the announcement themselves on Monday.

After the ecstatic couple had driven away, Carol set about to organize Edith's things so it would be easy for her to collect them on Monday. Her mind turned to thoughts of what married life would be like. As was her habit, she immediately told the Lord, "Whatever You want, Lord. I want Your will. If I could serve You better as Warren's wife, please show us. But if not, I'm content to serve you alone."

Carol was not long without a roommate, for summer vacation went quickly and fall semester began too soon. She roomed with a widow named Louise and campus life took on an entirely different aspect from the year before. Mary and Edith both lived close by, but there was little time to visit either of them once school began. Carol missed her long talks with Warren, but, true to his promise, he wrote her frequently. She answered faithfully.

By December Warren began including more of his feelings for Carol in his letters. The week before Christmas, Carol was not surprised to receive a package in the mail. Of course, everyone who knew of the situation wanted to see her open her gift, but Carol confined the grand unveiling to herself and Louise.

Setting down her books and taking time to remove her sweater, Carol prolonged the moment. Louise could hardly stand it.

"What do you think it is?" she finally asked Carol.

"Well, it's two boxes, by the shape of it."

Carol hung up her sweater and closed the closet door.

"Aren't you just dying to open them?" Louise asked. "How can you be so calm?" She sat down on her chair and scooted it over toward the desk where Carol picked up the package.

"Oh, my!" Carol exclaimed, as she tore the outside wrapper off.

"That does look like a ring box," Louise whispered, edging closer.

Carol sat down and carefully opened the tiny box. There, snuggled into a red velvet lining, lay a sparkling diamond ring.

"Were you expecting this?" Louise wanted to know.

"I'm not surprised," she answered thoughtfully. "Yes, I guess you could say I was expecting it." Her eyes twinkled and she could not keep from smiling.

"Oh, I'm so happy for you," Louise squealed, hugging Carol. "Warren is a fine Christian man. You two belong together."

Then she stopped and held Carol at arm's length. "You are going to say 'Yes' aren't you?"

Carol finally laughed. "Of course. I've been praying that if it is God's will for Warren and me to serve Him together in India He would show Warren. This must be God's answer."

Carol pondered the ring a few minutes, turning it this way and that in the light. Then she took it out and placed it on her finger. "Now the whole world will know we're engaged," she said, as she continued to inspect the diamond from every angle.

"There is another box," Louise prompted, her curiosity once more getting the best of her.

Carol turned to open the larger box. The other gift would be an afterthought now. She slipped the wrapper off a box of candy, and found a letter from Warren tucked inside. But Louise was disappointed if she expected Carol to share the letter's contents with her.

The happy couple planned to marry in a year and a half. Much as she hated being separated from him, Carol knew it was for their good that Warren attended school at a different Bible college, for her second and third year classes were more difficult than the first. She took her Christian service assignments seriously. Besides witnessing at the hospital she now taught children's classes.

Vacations were the only times she had to develop any social life, the only times she could be with Warren, but even then their work schedules kept them from spending much time together.

They discussed their plans and began setting aside money for the wedding during the few times they had together in the summer vacation between Carol's second and third years of Bible training. Once more they parted so Carol could finish her studies at PBI and Warren at Westmont. Carol continued making her plans. They had a limited amount of money set aside for the wedding and, with her family so far away, she had only her friends at school to help her. This worried her. Then her feelings about being married to Warren became uncertain.

"It isn't that I don't love him," she told the Lord one night. "I'm not sure what it is. Maybe it's because we don't see each other often. I guess I'm disappointed he isn't the one who brings up our serving You in India."

She stopped to contemplate her feelings about what she had just prayed. Then she went on.

"Lord Jesus, I thought this was Your will. Now I'm confused. Just lead me."

They continued planning and Carol kept asking the Lord to work in both of their lives. As her confusion grew, her daily prayer became, "Lord, if it's not Your will, please do something to stop our wedding, because I don't want to be out of Your will. I want to serve You. If it's Your will for me to be in India, that's where I want to be."

On the morning before their wedding date, Carol's Bible reading schedule took her to Psalm 30. Verse five caught her attention. She wondered why God gave her such a verse the day before her wedding: "Weeping may endure for a night, but joy cometh in the morning." She meditated on that thought, then spent her usual time in prayer.

Carol had some last-minute errands to run concerning the wedding.

She visited with the friend who offered her flowers for the wedding and talked with Mary to calm her nervousness. It was early afternoon when she returned to her house and found Louise sitting on the couch, red-eyed as though she had been crying.

"Oh, Louise, what is it?" Carol cried. She set down her purse and noticed a telegram on Louise's table. "Is someone in your family sick?"

Louise could barely get the words out.

"No, my family's all right." She realized Carol saw the telegram paper. The tears began to flow again.

"What is it, then?" Carol demanded. "You'll have to stop crying and tell me."

"It's from Warren," Louise finally managed to speak through sobs.

"Is it to me?" Carol asked, picking up the telegram.

"No, he sent it to me," she answered. Then anger replaced sorrow. "He says to tell you the wedding is postponed."

Carol dropped into her chair, crumpling the telegram.

"Well, why didn't he send it to me?" she asked. Then, "I guess he didn't know how," she answered her own question.

"Oh, Carol, I am so sorry," Louise wailed, hugging her. "This must hurt you so much."

"Why, I'm not crying," Carol said, surprised at her own composure. "I think I'm disappointed. I'm sure I love Warren but I love Jesus more. I've been asking Him to stop this wedding if it isn't His will. Why cry when God has done what I asked?"

Louise shook her head and the sobs continued. She could not speak. Instead of comforting Carol, Carol comforted her by sharing with her the verse that God had given her that morning.

"How good to be sure of the leading of the Lord," she said, and that confidence continued to uphold her when the tears did come.

New arrivals to India, 1945

Chapter 4

TO THE REGIONS BEYOND

"Sure, I know all about being saved—if that's what you want to call it. Why, just a couple of years ago I got to hear that famous preacher—what's his name? Billy Sunday, yeh, that's it. I got to hear him preach."

"So, did you ask the Lord Jesus to be your Savior then?" Carol asked the man in the bus seat next to her.

"No! No need to! I'm just as good as the next guy. Why I'm as good as you are," the man bragged.

Carol silently asked God for wisdom. Before she boarded this bus to Los Angeles she'd asked the Lord to give her a chance to witness to someone. Now here was her chance. This man needed the Lord.

"I used to think that too," Carol went on. "Then I read in the Bible that all are sinners and come short of the glory of God. Everyone needs to be saved."

The conversation went on and on. The man did not mind talking about spiritual things, but he saw no need to be saved.

Eventually the darkness and the smooth rocking of the bus made Carol drowsy, so she settled herself for a nap.

At two o'clock in the morning the smooth rocking changed abruptly to disjointed wobbling, waking Carol instantly.

"What's happening?" she asked in alarm.

"Looks like the driver is trying to keep from running over that trailer up there," her seatmate answered.

Carol sat up straight and tried to see out the front window. The bus lurched from side to side, making it difficult to stay in her seat.

"I don't see a trailer," she complained.

"Neither did the driver, I guess. There aren't any lights on it. It appeared out of nowhere."

The lurching increased as the bus ran off the road, crashing into a dirt bank. Drowsy passengers awakened to their own screams as the bus bounced over the gravel shoulder and off the hillside. Carol clutched toward the back of the seat in front of her, missed, and fell into the aisle behind the driver. She looked up in horror to see her companion crashing through the front windshield.

Carol looked around to help someone, but the driver stopped her with a shout: "Please leave the bus immediately. Do not try to find your luggage. Walk to the exits and meet your traveling companions outside of the bus."

The babble of the frightened and injured increased with the sound of pounding as passengers closest to the doors tried to force them open. Carol wondered if they would be trapped inside. Would the wrecked bus explode?

"Stand away from the doors," the driver ordered. Just then someone on the outside kicked open the door nearest Carol.

As soon as she went outside Carol looked for her seat companion. He lay at the side of the road, covered with a blanket. Her training prepared her for his condition, but still she thanked God it was too dark to see clearly. Half of his face had been sheared off by the windshield.

Carol knelt and asked if she could do anything for him. No answer.

"Can you hear me?" Carol asked, gently laying her hand on his shoulder.

"Yes," came the faint response. He tried to turn his head toward her.

She knew an ambulance would be along with medics to care for his physical needs. Right now his spiritual needs were more important.

"Now is the time for you to accept the Lord into your heart, believe in Him and be saved," she blurted.

For several moments she sat by him, waiting for a response. Then her heart rejoiced to hear, "Thank you, Lord."

After a few minutes more he said, "I'm so cold."

Carol brought him another blanket from the emergency vehicle that arrived. Then she waited with him until medics came. When he was settled in the ambulance she boarded a waiting bus for Los Angeles, praying for him as she went.

Carol's heart was already turned toward India. She depended on the Lord to lead her as he had at Bible school and during her recent broken engagement. She worked at a hospital in Los Angeles for a few weeks until one day when she received an invitation from Beam and Edith Shaeffer to attend a summer Bible Conference at Mission Springs, a place farther north in the coastal hills of California. Craving Christian fellowship, she drove to the conference grounds. She prayed the Lord would use this time to direct her further.

Camp Director Bill Graves met her when she arrived at the conference grounds.

"So nice to get to know you, Carol," he grinned, pumping her hand. "I've heard so much about you from Beam and Edith."

"Well, I hope it's been good that you heard," Carol answered. She had not expected so hearty a welcome.

"I've heard that you want to serve the Lord, and that's enough for me," he went on. Then, as if an afterthought, "Say, would you like to be our camp nurse? We could use one."

"Why, I'd be glad to," Carol answered, recognizing her opportunity to serve the Lord and get to know many of His people as well.

During the conference week Carol recognized Bill Graves as a man of faith. When the week ended, she returned with him and his family to the Vallejo Bible Church where he pastored. The church was newly organized and excited about missions. They voted to give Carol $25 a month to help in their children's outreach program and to continue giving that amount as the Lord led her out to the mission field. Within the next few months they incorporated as a church and Carol became one of the charter members.

In between children's classes, Carol spent time talking with Bill about how to get to the field of India. No new mission agencies were allowed into India, so they began to research the missions currently working there. Carol wrote to several agencies and she and the church prayed over each one. Eventually they felt God's leading to apply to The Evangelical Alliance Mission.

Carol wrote to TEAM, telling them she had been assured of God's call to India. She was ready to go. She waited for several weeks for their answer, checking the mail eagerly every day.

To her delight, the letter that finally arrived asked her to go to their headquarters in Chicago to meet with the board of directors. She had carefully hoarded her money for just such an opportunity. The church made up the difference with an offering for travel expenses. She left Vallejo in high hopes: she was on her way to India.

The knowledge of God's will gives great confidence so the stern-looking board members did not intimidate Carol. She knew God was sending her to India and she expected God to direct these men to help her get there. She did not know what to expect of the meeting, but she left with her head swimming: so many requirements to fulfill before she could go! But God had led her and she dutifully returned to Vallejo with the list of things she would need before she could depart: $50 a month support, $1000 for transportation, and a small "outfit": personal items she must have on the field. Even with these needs met, the board couldn't tell her when she'd sail for India. World War II was the nation's top priority and missionary transportation was limited.

The church at Vallejo took Carol's needs to the Lord as though they were their own. Carol didn't know anything about doing deputation, but she did know how to pray. God honored that. Other churches began to hear about her and asked her to share her burden with them. Gradually pledges of support began to come in.

She knew what to do with the first offering she received. This small amount could grow in a bank account until she had the needed $1000. Always eager to share what the Lord was doing in her life, she praised the Lord and explained to the banker what the account would be used for.

"That's impossible," he laughed. "Nobody's going to give you $1000 to go to India as a missionary."

His words hurt but Carol reminded herself that the world's people couldn't understand God's workings. As the money came in she faithfully reported to the banker how her funds were growing. Soon he had to admit that he couldn't understand it at all, but he had been wrong.

Raising the money was one thing; acquiring the "outfit" was something else. Because of the war many of the listed items were scarce. Carol would be in India for several years before she came back to the states, so clothing had to be purchased with that in mind. With amazement and gratitude she saw God touch people's hearts to deny themselves and give her their ration cards for the many pairs of shoes the mission required her to take.

In a few months Carol had her complete travel fund in the bank. She wrote to TEAM headquarters and they suggested she come to Chicago for two months of training. Once more she left Vallejo in excitement with the promise that God's people would continue praying for her. In Chicago she enjoyed learning all she could about India and the missionaries who were already serving the Lord there. But when the two months had passed she was again disappointed: passage to India was still not available.

Whatever ship she did take would leave from New York, so she chose not to return to far away California. Instead she waited at her sister's home in Washington, D. C. The days dragged but she used the time to get reacquainted with her sister and to witness to her sister's family and others she met. Every time the telephone rang, Carol hoped it would be the mission, telling her she could go. Every day's mail brought the same anxiety.

At last the telephone call came: "You have passage on a troop ship to India. We can't tell you exactly what day. That's a military secret, but they will notify you."

Chicago had been a busy city, but New York was even busier, especially during wartime. Carol was glad her sister's father-in-law helped her find a hotel room to stay in until the military notified her of the departure date.

So many delays, but departure day finally came. Carol boarded the vessel and discovered she shared a hospital room cabin with thirteen other people, some of them missionaries from other agencies. The crowded condition gave them opportunity to exhibit the Christian life, but the group soon found this was no luxury cruise. They stood at tables to eat out of tin plates and drink from tin cups, military style. They seldom had fresh water for baths, and often had to clean the filthy bulkheads (bathrooms) before they could use them. Carol praised God for the strength to live in such surroundings and she thanked Him for the lessons she learned, knowing they would benefit her in India.

In a few weeks they landed in Egypt where they stayed in a British army camp for 11 days. Compared to the troop ship, this was like a vacation. They even had the opportunity to visit the pyramids and a museum. When it came time to continue their journey, the group of non-military passengers split. Carol's group boarded an Indian troop ship.

For the first time Carol saw Indian men, and they looked fierce. Their dark beards, knives and turbans frightened her. She reminded herself repeatedly of God's love for Indians drawing her to this land.

The closer they came to Bombay, the more excited Carol became. The night before docking, she could neither sleep nor eat. At daylight she headed for the rail so she would miss none of the activity. Although she especially wanted to see the Gateway of India, she forgot to look for it when she saw throngs of people either unloading the ship or meeting the returning servicemen. God brought to her mind Exodus 23:20: "Behold, I send an angel before thee, to keep thee in the way, and to bring thee into the place which I have prepared."

In the midst of gathering and repacking their belongings, the group of missionaries was interrupted by an Indian steward who summoned them to a meeting. Carol anticipated spending a week in Bombay, contacting the mission station and maybe doing some sight-seeing, at least learning to get around a little in the foreign land. The travel agent from the Intermission Business Office changed those plans.

"You'll have to leave Bombay tonight," he told them. "Mission- aries fleeing China have come through Burma and are arriving. All the hotels are filled. We expect they will continue to be filled until these people obtain passage to the United States."

The shipmates tried to encourage one another, but Carol could not control the horror on her face. She did not know how to travel in a foreign country. She could not communicate with the Indian people. She did not know the way to the mission station, nor could she read the signs.

A flood of despair washed over her mind, followed instantly by a flood of God's peace. "My presence shall go with thee, and I will give thee rest," He seemed to say. God had not brought her this far to abandon her.

The travel agent took the group of missionaries who needed to make reservations to the railway station. From there Carol telegraphed the mission station at Amalner to let her coworkers know she would arrive at 9:30 the next morning. Then she bought a mosquito net and helmet and in late afternoon she boarded the train to a town called Jalgaon where she would have to transfer to a train going to Amalner.

Carol thanked the veteran missionary friend who told some coolies to take care of her luggage and see that she got on the right train at Jalgaon. She did not know whether to trust these young Indian boys or not, but relaxed when she realized she had no choice. God was in control and early the next morning, true to their word, they helped her make the change at Jalgaon.

On the second train Carol shared a coach with three Indian women wearing beautiful, bright colors. They spoke no English. She did not know which of the many Indian languages they might speak, even if she had known any of them. They communicated with Carol by smiling and pointing.

As soon as the train began moving the three Indian women took out their breakfast. They saw Carol had brought nothing to eat, so they offered her a "dish"—a leaf. They put rice and something yellowish on it. Carol knew she would have to get used to Indian fare so she followed their example and ate from the leaf. After showing her how to eat, her companions watched for her reaction.

"Wow! This is spicy," Carol thought to herself, but she smiled and nodded her head. Her companions laughed and jostled one another as they began to eat from their own leaves. After the first shock of spiciness, Carol decided she liked the taste. In this strange foreign country, at least she found the food enjoyable.

If Carol was curious about her companions, they were every bit as curious about her. They watched her and pointed back and forth from her hands or face to her legs. At first Carol didn't understand what troubled them. Finally one of them crossed the coach to sit beside her and began plucking her stockings out from her legs to inspect them. Carol laughed with them. She imagined them going to their homes that evening telling all about riding the train with the strange foreigner who wore funny stockings that made her legs look brown while her hands and face were a pasty white.

The ride from Jalgaon to Amalner took only one hour. Carol didn't know the way and she didn't trust the conductor to announce the stations. Sometimes he announced them and sometimes he didn't. She watched the signs, which were written in Marathi and English. Finally she saw "Amalner" written in English so she hurried to gather her belongings.

"It's a good thing the English sign was there," she said to herself, for the conductor had indeed neglected to announce where they were.

Once off the train she felt a rising panic fearing the train would leave before she could find her luggage. With relief she recognized her fellow missionaries taking care of the luggage for her. They had received her telegraph just a half hour before!

More surprises followed. Carol visualized herself living in a little shack, but her new friends took her to a large white house, the mission headquarters building. Here she would learn the Marathi language, but first they put her to bed where she stayed until she got over her first contact with amoebic dysentery, picked up in Egypt.

Evangelistic touring team
(Carol on left)

Chapter 5

BEYOND THE ROADS

Beyond the roads were jungles—jungles filled with tigers and panthers. Carol needed no one to caution her about wandering out there by herself.

Yet out in the jungle clearings were the villages—villages filled with people who needed to hear about Christ, the true and living God. For these needy people God brought Carol to India. Because of their many idols, false and dead, the Lord Jesus Christ must be presented as the true and living God.

To reach these villages the missionaries drove a jeep to the end of the road, then walked to the villages beyond. As soon as Carol finished her orientation in the big white mission station house, she went out with the ministry teams to these far-off villages. She wondered if there was an end to the villages in the regions beyond the roads. As they progressed from village to village, back into the rugged mountains, Carol often thought, "Now! We have reached the last village in Kalvan area." She knew they had never reached the last person for Christ—but surely there were no more villages beyond that point.

Then, as they came to each "last village," the nationals would always point to at least one more. She was happy to give a gospel witness and to hand out Scripture portions in each place, along with whatever medical services the people needed.

When the gospel teams did not go out, Carol worked in the mission clinic. Often she served in place of a doctor. She soon learned to depend on the Lord to diagnose and treat many unusual ailments.

One morning as Carol made her rounds in the clinic, a commotion outside caught her attention. A villager stumbled into the clinic compound shouting strange words Carol couldn't understand.

It sounded like he said, "Come quickly! Come quickly! My wife has lost her inside luggage!"

Carol ran to meet him at the clinic doorway.

"Calm down! Now tell me again, slowly," Carol said as she reached his side. The language was still unfamiliar to her and she felt she must not have had heard correctly.

"Come! You have to come! My wife has lost her inside luggage!" he repeated, more slowly, but his eyes rolled in terror. His whole body shook from the exertion of running so far.

Carol didn't understand his problem, so she couldn't decide how to prepare. There was no sense in wasting time trying to figure it out, so she gathered some basic supplies and called for someone to drive the jeep. In a few minutes they started along the rough 30 miles to the man's village.

Fortunately the road led all the way to this village. By midmorning they arrived in a flurry of dust. Scrambling after the Indian man, she slipped out of her sandals at the door and bent down to enter his hut. Her eyes took a moment to adjust to the dimness as he led her to a low, darker room in the back of the little house. There she found a small woman lying on the floor with a dirty rag carefully draped across her stomach. Without a word Carol knelt by her. Lifting the rag, she found a pile of intestines lying on her abdomen.

Carol's mind whirled: "What do I do now? The nearest hospital is 80-90 miles away. The rough roads will shake more intestines out of the abdominal cavity causing her death. She is set for peritonitis from the present contamination. Is there hope to save her? What if she dies on the way—the jeep isn't an ambulance. The roads aren't paved: just rough rocky ruts. Is it right to take her from her home where she can die with her family around her? But most of all, is she ready to meet God, the One she heard so little about?"

The family needed no direction. Of course—she must go to the hospital. They began making preparations to transport her. First they filled the back of the jeep with straw, then covered the straw with a quilt. In that small place they would lay the patient and her family members would squat all around her.

It would do no good to argue with them, so while the family busied themselves with the jeep, Carol took care of the patient. She soaked clean cloths in boiling salt water. As she worked she used the opportunity to explain John 3:16 to the patient.

"God so loves you," she said, wringing out a cloth and gently placing it on the woman's intestines.

The woman winced and then relaxed as she felt the warmth of the cloth. Carol saw that now the woman could concentrate better on what she was saying to her.

"God so loved you that He gave His Son to save you—to give you eternal life," she explained as she placed another warm cloth. The woman's eyes showed understanding.

Carol brought a dry cloth and placed it over the soaked ones. The woman looked frightened, but Carol explained, "Now, I have to bind this tight so you don't lose any more 'luggage' on the way."

Her patient relaxed again under Carol's skillful hands.

"You know this life is short," Carol went on.

"Mine might be even shorter," the woman finally whispered.

"But nothing could be better than eternal life with God," Carol assured her.

She winced again as Carol lifted her to tighten the binding cloth. "Let's pray before they load you into the jeep," Carol said. The woman shut her eyes while Carol asked God for a safe journey and that the woman would live to receive Jesus as her Savior.

At Carol's "amen" the husband came in to carry his wife out to the jeep. He placed her on the quilt and all of her family scrambled in and found places around her. Carol and the driver climbed into the seats and began the bouncy trip to the hospital.

There was no time to stop and see to her patient's suffering, but Carol watched and prayed most of the four hours it took to get to the hospital. The woman lingered near death when they finally stopped and lifted her out of the jeep, but she raised her head enough to smile at Carol.

News traveled slowly throughout the territory. Carol knew when she left the woman at the hospital she may not hear news of her recovery or death. Finally, after several weeks, she learned her patient not only survived the jeep trip and the surgery but also the tiny Indian lady had responded to God's love.

Ready for a bullock cart ride to go shopping
(Carol on right)

A poorer Indian home

Headquarters in India

Traveling by camel

Chapter 6

THE OXCART AND THE TIGER

"Virginia, this has been the most exhausting day of my life," Carol said to her partner. "I'll be glad to get back to the tent to collapse."

"What? No dinner? You should have worked up a good appetite out here in the clinic," Virginia laughed.

"Oh, no. Someone's waiting," Carol groaned as the jeep bounced down the makeshift road to the front of her tent. Reluctantly she pulled her weary body from the driver's seat.

The waiting man recognized the two women as nurses. Instantly he arose from squatting on the ground and rushed toward them.

"You must come!" he pleaded. "My wife. Her baby will not come!"

Carol had seen the problem before. But she was weary. Maybe if it were not far away. She needed time to think.

"Where do you come from?" she asked.

Carol's spirits fell as he described the last village beyond the end of the road—thirty miles away.

"Oh, I cannot. I am too tired," she answered, leaning back against the jeep.

Virginia had stayed long enough to hear the man's request. Then she went to find the evangelist. Carol turned toward her tent and the man stepped in front of her.

"I have waited all day," he wailed. "My wife will die. There is no hope." He began to weep.

Truly sorry for him, but so tired she knew she could not help him, Carol squeezed by him to enter her tent and plopped down on her cot to pray. The Lord knew she had no strength for such a trip, at night, through the jungle, after a very hard day. The task seemed beyond any possibility. Her mind kept saying, "I won't be able to go; I simply can't go!"

Carol heard the man weeping. He arrived at the tent early in the morning waiting all day for Carol to come. Now she refused to help and all seemed hopeless to him.

As Carol prayed, the evangelist came in and interrupted her. He tried to explain the desperate condition of the woman who was momentarily expecting to deliver a baby.

Wearily Carol explained, "I'm not insensitive to the woman's needs; it is just beyond my strength. Look at me! I am already exhausted. How could I drive the jeep over those rough roads? How could I walk the eight miles beyond that and then deliver a baby? There's no way I can do it, even though I want to."

"Carol, I understand. You have no strength but God has all strength. Can we pray together about it?"

"Of course," Carol answered. During the prayer Virginia slipped into the tent and joined them. Carol felt the Lord wanted her to go, assuring her of His boundless strength available to her.

They arose from their knees then the evangelist spoke to the Indian man. "The nurses will come, but first they must eat," he explained.

The man nodded. He understood their need for strength, but he paced impatiently while waiting. Carol and Virginia ate supper then found Emmanuel, a young Christian, to drive for them.

In the midst of her weariness, Carol felt God's strength through a memorized verse. Once they settled into the jeep, Carol shared it with all of them. 2 Corinthians 12:12: "Therefore, I take pleasure in infirmities, in reproaches, in necessities, in persecutions, in distresses for Christ's sake; for when I am weak, then am I strong." She told them how these last words especially spoke to her.

The journey took several hours through black darkness. Tall grass grew on each side of the ruts, hiding the road. Carol wondered if this was the first jeep to travel that route. It would have been easy to worry about unseen rocks or tree trunks between the ruts, which could bring disaster to the jeep and its occupants, but she trusted the driver. They advanced slowly with frequent stops to inspect the road. At one point the road became very rutted and the jungle seemed to close in on them. Everyone got out to look at the road when suddenly Emmanuel called out, "It's all right! Nothing wrong here! Let's get going!"

They scrambled into the jeep and sped off. Carol wondered about the sudden hurry, but said nothing. "Emmanuel must be impressed with the Indian man's great need," she thought.

Soon the road became impassable. They decided to borrow an oxcart in the small, nearby village. The patient's husband quickly made the arrangements then they started out once more.

Oxcarts are not luxury vehicles! A quilt helped little to pad the bumps as they jounced over rocks and ruts. When one corner of the cart jabbed Carol in the back she moved to get more comfortable. Then a sudden bounce slammed her arm into the cart's side. As she shifted her position to protect her back and her arm the lurching cart made her bump her leg. Although someone suggested they drive slowly and carefully, Emanuel increased the speed, compounding the bumps and bruises. Between bounces and bumps Carol noticed Emmanuel frequently look back, as though something or someone followed them.

Finally they arrived! The Indian man scurried from the cart to provide a basin of water for them to wash their hands and feet. As soon as she finished washing, the man hurried her to the small room where his wife lay.

There was neither time nor place for intercessory prayers, but she and Virginia carried on a constant heart-prayer for her as they proceeded. They knew Emmanuel was praying as he waited. As God's promises came to mind they claimed them for this desperate woman.

Carol immediately examined the patient and found her condition more serious than she imagined. The local midwives did what they could, but their efforts killed the baby. The mother needed immediate hospital care, but Carol and everyone else knew that was impossible. Carol had to do whatever she could for the woman.

She thanked the Lord for the special obstetrical training she had received during her first furlough but that training in itself was not enough. Her mind filled with possible complications, the worst being the mother's death.

After examining the woman, Carol met with the family for a few minutes. She paused for a moment, then said, "The baby is not alive." Their eyes told her they had already guessed that. A brother at the husband's side reached out to comfort him.

Carol continued, "We will have to pull the baby from the mother." Before they had time to wonder how that would be done, she showed them the large forceps she intended to put on the baby's head for the delivery. The relatives nodded agreement to this solution.

As Carol worked with the patient, Virginia helped in the preparation. She set the small instruments to boil over an open fire, then looked for a way to boil the large forceps. Someone in the family brought a tall copper water vessel. At her direction they filled it with water then set it to boil. While it boiled, Virginia looked for thick cloths to use as pot holders. She almost despaired of ever finding anything when she saw a large cloth hanging over the shoulder of a man warming himself at the fire.

"Just the thing," she cried, facing the man. She pointed to the needed cloth.

"Will you let me use your cloth to lift the pot?"

The man was happy to be able to help. When he began to unwind it, Virginia realized it was part of his dhoti, the pantslike garment Indian men wear.

"No! No! Don't do it!" Virginia gasped.

Ignoring her objections he calmly continued, unwinding until dressed in his shirt and loincloth, the customary garments of the Kakani tribesmen.

By now, most of the townspeople stood inside and around the door. When all was ready, Carol asked the men to leave the room. She allowed some of the women to remain. The patient's husband asked to stay. With some misgiving Carol allowed him.

Carefully Carol placed the forceps around the dead baby's head. Maneuvering them exhausted her tired arms. When she tried to pull the baby out, no strength was left in her arms for the delivery. Now she knew why she let the patient's husband stay in the room. She needed his strength. He responded eagerly.

"Sit behind me. Pull on my arms when I tell you," Carol directed. "Be sure you let go when I nod my head."

He nodded his own head, indicating he understood.

Together they pulled. Carol thanked the Lord for the man's strength. The baby's head emerged. She nodded for the man to stop pulling, allowing her to finish the delivery. He was so excited he continued pulling. Carol feared there might be more damage done to the mother, but the few resulting complications were minor.

When the dead baby was born Carol heard the women in the room murmuring their gratitude.

The husband shared his relief with Carol as she finished ministering to the woman. "This was her first baby. We have no others."

"I am so sorry. It looks like she'll not be able to have a child," Carol told him.

He remained quietly at her side for a few moments. Then he said, "A man needs children. I will have to get another wife. But I love this woman. I will take care of her, because I love her, although I cannot keep her for a wife."

After Carol and Virginia finished putting away their instruments and supplies the neighbor women brought them some food. They left the village in the oxcart just as the sun rose. As they jounced over ruts and rocks they held a praise meeting.

Emmanuel spent some of the night hours sleeping, so he attacked the job of driving with renewed vigor. As they bounced along Carol compared his actions to the night before.

"It is easier to drive an oxcart in the daytime," she remarked.

"Oh, yes," he laughed. "And safer."

"You mean because of the rocks and ruts?" Virginia asked.

A strange look crossed his face, then he decided to share his concerns with them.

"The rocks and ruts could hurt us, but not as much as the tiger following us last night!"

"So that was the problem!" Carol and Virginia laughed together. It was easy to laugh about it in the sunshine.

Carol added. "No wonder God gave me Isaiah 12:2 to think about. 'Behold, God is my salvation; I will trust, and not be afraid; for the Lord, even the Lord is my strength and my song; He also is become my salvation.'"

Bringing water

Chapter 7

PERSECUTED BUT PROTECTED

"Now that we have a Bible institute in the area, we will be able to reach out to the villages with the Gospel more often," Carol spoke to the student evangelist riding next to her in the jeep.

"It's good experience," he agreed. "Good for us to put our learning into practice and good for the villagers to hear the Gospel."

"Well, here's Avana," Carol said as she guided the jeep to a cleared area near the center of the village.

Quickly she, the student, Evangelist Shivaji and the Bible woman who had been riding in the back, jumped down from the jeep and began unpacking materials for the evening's meeting. The second jeep pulled up behind theirs and did the same.

Shivaji stopped to look toward the setting sun.

"You young fellows go around the village with your literature and Gospels, while the rest of us set up for the meeting," he directed. "That should generate more interest while it is still daylight."

In a few minutes the students returned.

"It's a small village, but they took most of our tracts and Gospels," one exclaimed. "Let's hope our good reception continues."

As the shadows darkened, the missionaries used the sound system to draw villagers to the town center. Carol usually enjoyed singing Gospel songs with the team, but as soon as the service began she felt uneasy. In a few minutes she guessed why.

Between songs she heard Evangelists Shivaji and Sakharam whispering to each other.

"Maybe we should have planned a daytime meeting for Avana," Sakharam said.

"I see what you mean," Shivaji answered.

Carol followed his gaze. Several young men were lighting a fire near the back of the crowd. The evening was warm but they pretended to warm their hands. At first Carol couldn't understand what the commotion was about. On their makeshift platform one of the students began to give his testimony, so she turned her attention to him. Then it occurred to her. Those young men were burning the Bible portions they had received from the students that afternoon. The student giving his testimony continued as though nothing were wrong, but people near the fire began making noise and laughing at their antics. An Indian "holy man" in a green robe joined the men at the fire, encouraging their mockery.

Undeterred, Shivaji asked the Gospel group to find places to sit, then he began his sermon. Most of what he said could not be heard above the heckling from the fire area. He cut his sermon short and decided against showing the filmstrip on the life of the Lord Jesus Christ. It would be dangerous to turn out all the lights with this mob.

As the evangelist dismissed the meeting, Carol's fear mixed with sadness. This might be the last opportunity some of these villagers would have to hear the Gospel. She was sorry to see the meeting cut short. Most of the villagers slowly began wandering toward their homes while the missionaries gathered their equipment and worked together loading it into the luggage trailer. They all kept their attention on the young hecklers. Sure enough, the young men began to get in the way of loading the equipment.

"Please allow me to put these things into the jeep," one of the students politely asked.

The young man standing between him and the jeep laughed and gave the student a push. The other men laughed as the student fell, scattering his box of equipment. The evangelists rushed to help the student. The other young villagers began pushing the missionaries standing nearby.

"Let's go," Sakharam shouted to the rest of the missionaries.

As Carol ran toward the jeep she felt clods of dirt pelting her. "If only this town had lights," she thought. She knew they could not put the pressure lantern into the jeep without taking a chance on someone getting burned by it. If they put it out, the townsmen would become even more bold.

The Bible woman, Shivaji, and Carol scrambled into the jeep and sped through the large village gate as the first stone broke the back window.

"Oh, my! What about the rest of them? What about Sakharam?" Carol worried aloud.

"I can still see Virgi's lantern—no, it's out now!" the Bible woman answered.

"We'll have to wait for them up here," Carol answered, bringing the jeep to a stop beyond the town.

Their troubles were not over. A mob appeared behind them bombarding the jeep with stones. By the time Carol started the jeep moving again the townspeople had broken all the windows except the windshield. As they sped away Carol felt a glass pane glance off her neck, but the folds of her Indian garment protected her.

Farther on they stopped again and the other jeep roared up to their side. Gratefully, they watched the crowd disperse.

Carol, always the nurse, asked, "Now, who needs medical attention before we get back to the station?"

The students and evangelists looked each other over. Not one of them had been injured! With rejoicing they started the jeeps and made their way back to the station.

They arrived in the middle of the night but awakened everyone in the compound to join them in a praise service for the Lord's protection. Shivaji read Matthew 5:11-12. Each gospel team member rejoiced to be counted worthy to suffer for the Lord.

Their troubles with Avana did not end there. Because the village sat beside a main road, they often drove past it. In spite of their bad treatment there, the missionaries continued to pray that the villagers would accept the Gospel.

One day Carol and an evangelist had to drive in that direction. They were discussing their burden for the village. Suddenly a nine-year-old girl ran out and stood in the middle of the road, forcing Carol to stop the jeep. Carol asked her to move. To her surprise the child ran to Carol's window and jabbed at her face with a hand sickle.

Carol ducked. The evangelist jumped out, ran around to the girl, and pulled her arm back.

"Drive ahead!" he shouted to Carol. Carol obeyed then turned back to watch him scolding the girl. She noticed with sorrow that the child's hardened face did not respond in any way to the words of the evangelist.

Avana's antagonistic attitude continued. Carol prayed much for them. She thought there must be someone in the town who wanted to hear the Gospel. She could not believe everyone in the town was completely controlled by Satan.

One day she was called to Avana to minister to a sick old man who suffered with cancer of the cheek and throat. The Lord gave her courage to reenter the village, but her heart sank when she examined the patient. She yearned for an opportunity to overcome the town's hatred.

Praying the townspeople would not take it as further reason to reject her and the Gospel, Carol sadly told the man, "I'm so sorry. I don't have anything that can help you."

The patient turned away in despair. What could she do?

"I don't see any way for this to get better, but the government hospital can at least give you something to relieve your pain and suffering. Would you like me to take you to Nasik?"

The man nodded his head and his family agreed. At least he would not suffer so much.

Still the hardened villagers did not respond. For fifteen years Carol continued to pray for Avana. Then another group from the Bible Institute came to do practical work in their area. These young men traveled by bicycle, spending two weeks going from village to village, distributing tracts and selling Gospels. They sold them, rather than giving them away, so the Indians would value them enough to read them.

One day two of the student evangelists took their literature to Avana. Carol did not tell them of her previous experiences there because she hoped God had worked in the people's hearts so now they would be ready to listen to the Gospel.

She waited for the evangelists to return with their report, but once again the village of Avana drove the Christians from their town.

"They wouldn't let us give them any tracts," one student complained.

"At least they didn't buy your Bibles and then make a fire of them," Carol commented. "It's just like Jesus warned the disciples about in Matthew 10:14: 'And whosoever shall not receive you, nor hear your words, when ye depart out of that house or city, shake off the dust of your feet.'"

Years later, when Carol left India, Avana had not changed. The Gospel is truly a savor of life unto life to the saved and death unto death to those that perish. (2 Corinthians 2:15-16.)

Chapter 8

TERROR BY NIGHT

"Sakora! We do pick the tough towns," Carol commented.

"Yes," Evangelist Jayaont agreed. "However, we won't be visiting the village until next spring. Right now we need to prepare for nine boys who will be coming to the Boarding Home for this school year."

"Why would people in a town like that send their boys to us?" Carol's helper Vati asked. "All my life I've heard that village is Satan's stronghold."

"Thievery, violence...," Carol shook her head.

Jayaont interrupted. "Apparently that kind of life is fine for the adults, but some of the parents are looking for a better life for their children. Our reputation is becoming known, if only as a place where young men can get a good education. Let's pray these boys will find Christ as their Savior and through them we can reach their families."

The mission group did pray for the boys, not just that day but all the days thereafter.

The next week nine Sakoran boys came to the Christian Boarding Home. For the first time in their lives, they heard about Jesus Christ, the true and living God. The daily teaching, combined with the love shown by the teachers and other mission workers, began to have an impact in the lives of some of the boys.

Seko Athambe secretly believed what the missionaries taught him, but his faith met testing. He heard that his mother stepped on a poisonous thorn and her foot had swelled to a huge size. Seeking relief, she and her husband made the long trip to a famous "holy man" healer for special treatment.

"Go home and find a lemon," the "holy man" told her. "As soon as you arrive home, throw the lemon as far as you can. That will ensure you quick recovery."

A dedicated Satanist, she blindly followed the prescription but found no relief.

When Seko heard the news he encouraged his mother to come to the clinic for treatment and, to his surprise she did, staying for several days. The first morning she was there, Carol came outside the clinic to find her soaking her foot in hot water.

"Please, the hot water is not good for it," Carol cautioned. "Let me give you these antibiotics for it."

Seko's mother took the medicine, but refused to remove her foot from the hot water. Several times during the day Carol found her soaking her foot again. As Carol predicted, the swelling got worse. The next morning Carol again found her soaking her foot.

"Please, at least soak it in cool water," Carol pleaded.

"No, it needs to be hot," the mother answered.

Carol shook her head, but no amount of arguing changed the woman's mind.

"Here is more medicine," Carol offered.

"No, the swelling is worse. Your medicine is no good."

"It needs time to work," Carol explained.

"It needs a shot, like you gave that woman yesterday."

"A shot won't help," Carol replied. "Take this medicine. It's made for your problem."

"No, if you won't give me a shot, at least wrap it with herbs," the patient continued.

Carol turned away. How like salvation. So often we want to do it our way instead of taking God's prescribed remedy. The patient refused her help and in a few days returned to Sakora.

Seko prayed for his mother and continued to ask her to consider the clinic's remedy, but whenever she returned to the clinic she refused their medicine and requested a "miracle cure" injection or a medicine wrap.

Seko's father always came to the clinic with her. He listened carefully to the Gospel the clinic workers shared with them. He readily agreed to allow the missionaries to pray for his wife. Sometimes she agreed too, but because she had given herself over completely to evil spirits, she always turned her back to the missionaries when they prayed.

Carol began to dread the days when Seko's parents came, for the clinic workers complained about how rudely the mother treated them when they wouldn't give her what she wanted. She still refused the medicine they offered her. Gradually their visits to the clinic became less frequent. One day Seko returned from a vacation to report his mother was crippled and no longer able to walk.

Seko himself was a happy-go-lucky boy who agreed with everything he learned at school. Yet his parents' influence kept him from outwardly accepting Christ as his own Savior.

When spring came the evangelistic team camped at Sakora for a week, visiting homes in the daytime and holding evangelistic meetings every evening. Satan made the work difficult, but God encouraged their hearts with a few interested villagers.

They visited the home of Seko's friend Akish, and his mother said, "Akish tells me Jesus Christ is the true God, and he believes in Jesus. He says Jesus loves us and He died for us. He says he is going to heaven and I am going to hell, where there is fire and suffering. Please tell me more."

Yet few others showed any response. What a hard lesson for the missionaries: people listened, but did not come to a place of decision. They ended each day more discouraged than the last.

Akish's mother eagerly listened each evening, but before she made a profession of faith the missionaries had to leave. The trouble began one evening, just before the evangelistic meeting, when clouds began to gather in the sky. Just as evangelist Jayaont started to speak about "King Ahab and Elijah" it began to sprinkle.

Silently Carol prayed, "Lord, you stopped the rain for three and a half years when Elijah prayed. You are Elijah's God. You can stop the rain now so these people can hear the way of salvation through Christ!"

God did just that. The rain stopped and Christ was presented as the only God and Savior. The villagers had a clear gospel message to think about as they returned to their homes.

The missionaries returned to their tents and Carol thanked the Lord for a warm cot and a waterproof tent. It still looked like rain outside.

As she began to doze off, God seemed to speak to her. "Ask Me for protection."

"We're safe here, Lord, with all the parents of the boarding boys, aren't we?"

Again the Lord urged her to pray. Psalm 34:7 came to mind: "The angel of the Lord encampeth round about those who fear him and delivereth them."

As she began to pray, a long, blood-curdling scream interrupted her. She yelled from her bed as she jumped up. But no answer came, just the continuing scream.

Then she heard running feet as men from the town gathered around the evangelist's tent next to hers. Jayaont had not yet retired for the night. He had been preparing visual aids for the next day when he decided to look outside. As he lifted the tent flap, before him stood a man with an ax raised, ready to bring it down on Jayaont's head. Behind the man stood two others, armed with sickles, ready to attack.

The three attackers quickly disappeared into the night when they heard the villagers running toward the tents.

The Lord sent His angels to deliver them. Psalm 91:5 was true. They had no need to fear for the terror by night, but they decided to return to the mission station the next day.

Although Akish claimed to believe in Jesus and even witnessed to his mother, his actual salvation came about later.

One hot day Carol was working at the clinic with all the doors and windows wide open. Vati came in the gate. They both heard the sound of a truck and some boys yelling out by the road.

Vati ran back to the road and shouted, "Come quickly! Come quickly!"

Carol ran to her and found Akish lying on the ground, writhing in pain, blood streaming from his head. He had been hit by a metal projection on the passing truck. It slashed a six-inch cut on the side of his head, just missing both his eye and his ear. The truck driver stopped the truck but stood helplessly by, wringing his hands.

The teacher who lived next door heard the commotion and jumped the fence, yelling, "Big Sister! Bring the jeep right away!" He bent to examine Akish while Carol ran to get the jeep.

They gently placed Akish in the back of the jeep. The teacher held an old sheet over his injury to stop the flow of blood. With the horn blaring they rushed Akish to the government hospital on the other side of town. They arrived as the doctor was about to leave to go to a temple where he would offer a goat to Umbabi, the nine-foot high goddess with eighteen arms.

The hospital staff rushed Akish into the operating room while Carol sped back to Sakora to get his parents.

"Oh, no!" his mother wailed. "Get his father, I cannot come alone."

Carol looked beyond her to where the father sat, dead drunk in the middle of the day.

What should she do now?

"Help him," the mother yelled, running to her husband and trying to lift him to his feet.

Carol ran to his other side, but he fainted at their feet.

The commotion brought neighbors to the front of their house. Suddenly, the mother ran to a neighbor and begged him to come to the hospital with her. At this the father raised himself and insisted on coming with them. With the neighbors' help they all scrambled into the jeep and dashed toward the hospital.

On the way back to the hospital they came upon the scene of the accident. The truck driver was still there.

"Here's where it happened," Carol explained.

"Is that the truck?" Akish's mother asked.

"Yes, the poor driver doesn't know what to do with himself," Carol answered, deftly guiding the jeep around the truck.

"That's him?" the father asked, rousing from his stupor. "Stop! I will beat him to a pulp!"

Carol understood his feelings, but kept driving to the hospital.
When they arrived at the hospital, Akish was still unconscious from
the anesthesia. His parents entered the room where he lay and they
began to wail because they thought he was dead.

"No, he is alive," Carol shouted over their voices. Even though the
hospital nurses came in and confirmed her words, the parents did not
believe them until Akish woke up.

Akish stayed on the critical list for several days before he began to
recover. When he saw where the pipe had hit him, he really understood
how God miraculously saved his life. After Carol explained the gash on
his head was near the temporal vein, Akish realized he could have died at
any time. He finally understood God's great love for him and he accepted
Christ as his own personal Savior.

Carol, a helper, and patients at the dispensary where she treated patients for seven years.

Cleaning ears

Chapter 9

NO DOCTOR AT THE HOSPITAL

"Too few doctors and too many patients," Dr. Klokke remarked to Carol at the end of a busy day.

"But God gives you a good sense of humor to help you handle it," she answered.

"I have to laugh," he chuckled. "I make so many mistakes trying to explain things to these people. If only I knew the language better."

"At least you're able to figure out what they need and prescribe the right treatment," she encouraged. She too felt exhausted as she thankfully returned the last surgical tool to its case.

The following day even Carol wondered at the testimony that had gone out concerning this good doctor. Very seldom did the native spiritists take advantage of the clinic, but this morning a witch doctor squatted patiently at the beginning of the line, waiting for the doctor to see him.

Dr. Klokke and the patient talked together for a few minutes after Carol brought him into the examining room. The patient held an arm across his stomach and squinted as he talked.

"I cannot understand what he is telling me," the doctor confided in Carol, "but I see he has a cataract that is ready for surgery." Carol nodded. That explained the squinting. She smiled as Dr. Klokke explained to the patient that he needed an operation. For once the witch doctor seemed to understand and he readily agreed. He wanted relief from his problem.

In a few days Carol helped Doctor Klokke unbandage the patient.

"I can see again!" he shouted. "This is wonderful!"

Dr. Klokke smiled. "That's what we hoped for," he said. "Now you may go back to your village."

As Carol helped the witch doctor find his possessions, she noticed he still held his arm over his stomach. Finally he called to the doctor and asked, "Doctor, when will I get medicine for my stomach ache. That is why I came to the clinic!"

So the easy case had not been so easy after all. A quick examination revealed the stomach problem and the witch doctor went back to his village able to see and with medicine for his stomach as well.

In the early days of the clinics, patients had to furnish all their own provisions and take care of their own cooking. The caste system did not allow them to eat each other's food.

The original clinics had mud floors. A bed consisted of four legs and a frame, with flat tape woven to act as a mattress. Dr. Klokke usually instructed recovering patients to stay in their beds, but they sometimes interpreted his directions in strange ways. Apparently, as long as some part of their body touched the bed, that fulfilled the requirement—in their minds.

One wintry morning Carol entered the clinic and immediately asked, "Do you smell smoke?"

Her helper sniffed.

"There's a fire somewhere," she agreed.

They began searching, following the smell to a bonfire built in the middle of the room.

"I have no blanket," the patient explained as the two nurses rushed up to him.

The unglassed windows allowed the wintry cold into the room, so Carol understood why he did what he could for himself. A pot of water boiled for tea, and he sat in the middle of his overturned bed which he had pulled up close to the fire.

Carol admired his resourcefulness, but insisted the fire be put out and the bed righted. Then she helped him back into the bed. Her helper found him a blanket to use until his family could bring one to him.

Several days later Dr. Klokke took time off for rest. Carol looked forward to his vacation with mixed emotions. She knew he needed the time to recuperate from his exhausting schedule. They often saw between 100 and 150 patients a day, working from early morning to nightfall. In his absence Carol had the responsibility of the entire clinic. She enjoyed the challenge of being in charge, but she felt the weight of responsibility.

As senior nurse her duties included the care of simple problems like itch, conjunctivitis, ear ache, worms, bruises and burns. While the doctor was on vacation she could send difficult problems to another missionary hospital eight hours away. She hoped there would be no emergencies that would require the eight hour trip.

"This is going to be one of those long, busy days," Carol assured her helper one morning.

"It's already been that," her good-humored helper laughed.

Carol handed some medicine to a patient and looked out the window for a moment while the next patient came into the room.

"Who is that?" she asked, waving toward the open window.

The other nurse stepped to the window for a closer look. The patient looked too and said, "Oh, he's been out there all morning. He doesn't want to get in line."

"I wonder what he wants," Carol said as she turned her attention to the patient in front of her.

As she prescribed a salve for the woman's injury, she looked out the window again where the same man continued walking around outside with his mouth hanging open.

"Don't bring anyone else in yet," Carol directed. "I'm going to see if I can help that man."

She hurried out to see why he delayed coming into the office.

"What's wrong? Can't you close your mouth?" Carol asked.

All he could say was, "Ah! Ah!" and shake his head.

"You will have to come inside. Let me have a look at you," she said, leading him into "Minor Surgery."

In a few minutes Carol gave him anesthesia and pulled his jaw back into joint. She then left him with a male nurse while she returned to the other waiting patients.

In the afternoon her jaw patient woke up, but the anesthesia made him vomit, snapping his jaw out of joint again.

Carol performed the treatment again, putting his jaw back into place. This time she tied his jaw shut and stayed close by to cut the bandage if he started to choke. He awoke more comfortably in the evening and by morning seemed able to return to his village.

Carol waited until the following day to let him go home. As she finished her last examination of his jaw, she asked him, "What happened to make your jaw go out of joint the first time?"

He answered, "Nothing! I was just bawling out my wife!"

On another occasion, when the doctor was away, five men came to be treated for tetanus. A sadhu, or holy man, had removed their tonsils—by gouging them out with his thumb nails. Tetanus is hard to treat. One of the men died, but with intravenous feeding, stomach tubes, and prayer, the other four recovered.

Sometimes emergencies rose beyond what Carol was supposed to handle. Late one afternoon a young boy came with a twelve-inch-long, Y-shaped cut on the inside of his arm.

"Oh, my," Carol exclaimed. "When did this happen?"

"Early this morning," his mother answered. "He fell out of a tree."

"Why did you wait so long?" Carol asked. She knew the boy had suffered greatly all day.

The mother shrugged. "We thought it would heal itself."

"Heal itself!" Carol thought. "If it heals itself it will be of no use to this young man."

She took her time examining the arm, asking the Lord what to do. If she sent them to the next hospital, they probably would not go. Even if they did, that would add another eight hours to the time it had already been since the accident.

But could she take care of it herself? Many times she had assisted the doctor by giving novocaine or by sewing up after surgery. She made up her mind. She had to do it all on her own.

"Hold him so he can't see what we're doing," Carol told her helper.

As soon as the boy was in position she gave him an injection of novocaine. He squirmed but the helper held him tight.

"Now you'll have to be still so I can work on you," Carol said.

She wondered how to do the stitches. Looking again at the cut she thought it resembled the jagged edges of a torn blanket. She might not know doctor's stitches, but she did know how to do a blanket stitch.

As she began the boy squirmed again. She waited until he settled down, but every time she began, he tried to see what she was doing.

"I think he's afraid you're going to cut his arm off," her helper suggested.

"Then, maybe we should let him watch," Carol answered. "Let's try it."

The helper released the patient. He immediately quieted so Carol could work on him. Carol saw a look of hopefulness return to his eyes as she finished stitching the ragged skin.

After several days, Carol changed the bandages. The cut had not healed perfectly, which was not surprising since it had gone more than eight hours unattended. A small infection developed. Carol treated it and prayed it would heal.

The problem did not end there. Satan repeatedly buffeted Carol's mind with fears. She felt the weight of the boy's suffering from the infection, and blamed herself for her ignorance. She pictured his arm useless, afflicted with gangrene, amputated. He could lose his life from it. Then what? She would be held responsible. What might his parents do? the government? She was a foreigner and could face persecution.

To add to her worry, she heard of a nurse under a different mission who mistakenly gave a patient quinine powder instead of epsom salts. When the patient died the missionary was arrested. Fortunately the patient's relatives recognized her anguish and caring attitude, so they refused to prosecute. The case was dismissed, but Satan used the incident to further disturb Carol's mind.

As she went to the Word of God for promises to counter-attack Satan, the Lord gave her Philippians 4:6-7. Her mind continually returned to the words "be anxious for nothing...doing everything by prayer...letting the peace of God rule your heart and mind." Nevertheless, for about a month worry ruled instead of peace.

In spite of her fears God used this time in the young boy's life. While he stayed in the hospital they treated him like a son until he was well enough to go home. Every time he returned to have his dressings changed their relationship grew. The evangelist taught him about the Lord Jesus Christ every day.

Eventually he regained full use of his arm. At the same time God's Word triumphed in Carol's heart, taking away her fears and bringing her His peace.

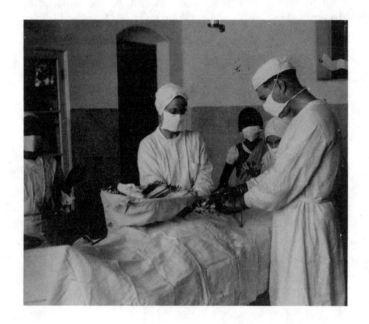

Dr. Klokke and Carol in the operating room

Chapter 10

TESTED AND TRIED

"Yes, they do look like leprosy!"

The doctor's words struck breathtaking fear to Carol's heart. Leprosy. Dreaded leprosy.

He ignored Carol's reaction, but continued to examine the spots on her arm as he spoke.

"We clinic workers meet a multitude of diseases—tuberculosis, cholera, typhoid, plague, hepatitis, and skin diseases like scabies and ringworm, as well as leprosy."

Carol could only nod. She'd seen them all but she never expected to be infected with the worst of them.

Returning to her room after the doctor's fearsome diagnosis, Carol sighed with gratitude that her roommate was not there. Her mind sorted through the steps that led to this day.

Last spring they had been busy with the evangelistic teams. Was it then that she first noticed the spots on her arm?

Yes, out in the villages with the gospel team, at the end of an exhausting day, when she took her sponge bath before falling into bed.

"Now, what?" she remembered asking herself, turning her arm for a better look.

"Well, there's no doctor here, but they look like ringworm to me," she said, drying her arm and pulling the case of medicines from under her cot.

Carol remembered thinking how she had not wanted to be bothered with "pesky ringworm." She applied a double dose of medicine then and on the following days. She wanted this problem out of the way in a hurry.

In spite of the strong medicine, the spots did not improve immediately.

"Maybe it's not ringworm," she remembered saying one night a couple of weeks later. She examined the spots carefully again.

"It might be eczema. I'll just treat it for both ringworm and eczema and get rid of it for sure," she said.

In another week she congratulated herself on her treatment. At least the soreness had gone away.

But the spots remained. She remembered checking them every evening. Then one day she noticed they were turning white. By the time the evangelistic teams finished for the year, Carol feared she had leprosy.

She remembered the courage it took to finally write to the mission doctor about her problem and ask for an appointment. As a nurse she described her ailment clearly and included her own fears, that it looked like leprosy to her.

Bringing her mind to the present, Carol reflected on her feelings that morning before the appointment. She could not even remember how she had prayed about it, but she knew that she had.

"Yes, they do look like leprosy!" The doctor's words repeated themselves in her mind as she tried to pray again. The one ray of hope was the analysis of the skin biopsy he sent to the laboratory at Miraj.

Daily Carol agonized in prayer over the report. At the end of two weeks she fearfully reported to her appointment to hear the lab report. She understood how busy the mission doctors were, but she had great confidence in their abilities, having worked beside them through many difficult cases.

The doctor opened Carol's medical record folder as he entered the examining room. He briefly scanned the lab report and said, "It could be the beginning of leprosy. We will start the treatment of dapsone."

Once again that terrible fear. Carol returned to her room and fell on her knees before the Lord, opening her Bible on the bed before her. For a long time she could do nothing but cry. Then God brought to her mind verses she had learned back in Bible institute: "Be strong and of a good courage...be not afraid...the Lord thy God is with thee...: (Josh. 1:9)." "Fear thou not for I am with thee: be not dismayed; for I am thy God: I will strengthen thee: yea, I will help thee; yea, I will uphold thee with the right hand of my righteousness. For I the Lord thy God will hold thy right hand...Fear not; I will help thee." (Isa. 41:10, 13.)

After a while Carol began to think clearly about her situation.

"Will I have to live at the leprosarium in Carvel, Louisiana?" she wondered. She could serve the Lord there but she knew God called her to India. "Is He changing the direction of my life?" she asked.

Then another thought struck. "I cannot stay here on the floor in this disheveled state. My roommate is having enough trouble just getting used to India. What a stumbling block I will be to her if I let her know about the leprosy."

She quickly bathed and prepared for the evening meal, thankful her roommate was working at the clinic while she had been at the doctor's office.

At dinner the medical aid who had taken her place that day asked her how she felt.

"I'll be fine," she answered, not wanting to share her problem with others. Later that night, alone in bed, she reflected on her answer and realized she could not share this problem with fellow workers. She would tell them the doctor made some tests and she didn't understand all about it. That was close to the truth.

Carol knew the only source of strength would be the Lord. She began to spend all of her free time praying and searching the Scriptures for promises of God's help and for facts about leprosy. She became impressed with how often leprosy typifies sin in the Bible.

"Oh, God," she prayed, "What a comfort it would be to share my burden with other missionaries. But I cannot, for they will surely think I am a great sinner to have gotten this terrible disease."

Each evening she noticed how raw her arm looked. "Thank You, Lord, for this long saree that covers the sores," she often prayed. She bandaged her arm when her roommate was not around. Then she dressed in her saree, a long bolt of bright fabric which she wrapped around her body then across her shoulder, neatly covering the affected arm. She wondered if she did the right thing or if she were needlessly exposing her roommate to the disease.

"Another problem, Lord," Carol prayed at the end of an exhausting day. "I don't want to shirk my share of the duties, but dapsone makes me feel so weak. Give me strength to serve you," she pleaded.

As the days continued Carol gave the Lord credit for unusual strength, in spite of her anemic condition. She continued to carry her heavy work schedule, refusing to take time off to go to another hospital for a second doctor's opinion. Besides, she had faith in the mission doctors' ability.

"Lord, I did not work well today," she confided in prayer one evening. "It is hard to concentrate on other people's ills when I have this overbearing problem of my own. Please give me peace about this. Help me to develop a servant's attitude in my heart. I did not come to India to center my life around myself."

God comforted her from His Word. Psalm 73:26 says, "My flesh and my heart faileth: but God is the strength of my heart, and my portion forever." Psalm 138:3 encouraged her: "In the day when I cried thou answeredst me, and strengthenedst me with strength in my soul."

For moment by moment strength and peace in the inner person, He gave her Philippians 4:6-7: "Be anxious for nothing; but in everything by prayer and supplication with thanksgiving let your requests be made known unto God. And the peace of God, which passeth all understanding, shall keep your hearts and minds through Christ Jesus."

After four months of treatment and inner struggle, Carol went to the hospital at Miraj for a follow-up exam. She no longer felt the panic she experienced when she came for the original diagnosis. She adjusted to living with the disease and learned to hide it well. The outcome of this appointment might change her service to the Lord, but He strengthened her for whatever lay ahead.

This doctor took another biopsy and thoroughly read the report while the laboratory workers made their analysis. Alone in the examining room, Carol searched God's Word and prayed. She thought, "I wonder if my life is to be filled with trips to the doctor from now on. I'd rather be the nurse than the patient."

After a while the doctor entered the examining room with a smile on his face.

"Whatever could this mean?" Carol wondered.

"According to this biopsy, you do not have leprosy!" he announced.

Carol could not believe what she heard.

"You mean it's cured?" she asked.

"No, it looks like you never did have leprosy. We can stop the dapsone and just let the spots heal by themselves."

What joy to find she did not have leprosy! Nor had she ever had it! She left the hospital bursting to share the great news, but she had hidden the problem so well no one knew.

With great relief she realized the disease no longer posed a problem but talking about it still did. Gradually she began to share her experience with fellow workers. She feared her supporters at home would pass it off as emotionalism, so she robbed herself of the joy of sharing this experience with them on her next furlough. Her audience might relate it to sin, so she left out this part of her life in her reports. She felt her struggles revealed a lack of spiritual victory and wondered if this testing might have been avoided if people had been faithfully praying for her. It was a circular argument she didn't know how to work out.

Eventually God's peace ruled her heart in this area.

During a staff devotion time after her return from furlough, Carol surprised herself by sharing what she learned.

"I guess you could call this my 'trial by leprosy'" she said. "At any rate it taught me more of the love of Christ."

"What do you mean," her roommate asked.

"I've learned to look at the plight of lepers with a different attitude—with understanding and compassion. There are so many beggars in India. Most of them are lepers. One of the hardest things for me to get used to in India was the crowds of them in the marketplaces, and the way they show off their disfigured limbs and faces."

"So how has your experience changed any of that?" another missionary asked.

"Oh, it hasn't changed them, but it has changed me. Now I don't avoid them. I try never to give them rupees without talking to them about the

Lord Jesus Christ. What an opportunity to share Bible verses about Jesus' healing lepers and forgiving sin. They need to see life as preparation for heaven, where we will have whole bodies!"

The other missionaries saw God's peace keep Carol's heart and mind. She showed a greater love for Christ and compassion for the lost. Younger missionaries heard about her life of faith and began coming to Carol for counsel. God brought her through tests to perfect her faith, to cause her to grow into the likeness of the Lord Jesus Christ. She wanted others not to fear partaking of His sufferings, that they might also partake of His joy.

Carol

Daily market

Chapter 11

BUBONIC PLAGUE IN PIMPALNER

"Mrs. Scarf is dying of cancer," the letter read.

"I know that," Carol answered. "We've been praying for our senior missionary for many weeks now."

She turned back to the rest of the letter.

"Esther and I are simply worn out with her care. We know she has little time left. Please come and take over for us during Mrs. Scarf's last days," Bea had written.

"Even her handwriting looks exhausted," Carol thought. "Yes, of course I will go. What an honor to be asked to care for this faithful missionary."

The mission office quickly gave their permission for Carol to take over the nursing duties at Pimpalner. A secretary made the travel arrangements. The next day Carol boarded a bus to begin the long trip. It was impossible to study on the bus, so Carol enjoyed the scenery as much as she could. In the late morning they drove through the area Carol had gone to with the gospel team last month. A village signpost reminded her of the time villagers had pelted their tents with rocks all night long. In the next village, natives had set fire to their tents. Carol remembered how God protected them by sending a sudden rainstorm that quenched the fire. She looked around at her fellow travelers.

"Always something to be on guard about in India," she reminded herself. "Tigers in the jungle and evil men in the city." She looked around for thieves.

In the crowded bus she had little to occupy her mind except the scenery and verses she had memorized. Her life verse came to mind: Philippians 1:20-21, "For me to live is Christ, and to die is gain. But if I live in the flesh, this is the fruit of my labor: yet what I shall choose I wot not."

"My life is yours, Lord," she prayed as another arm of the jungle passed her window. "By life or by death, I told you back in Bible institute. But there is so much death in India: am I to die here as a missionary, like Mrs. Scarf?"

At the next stop Carol transferred to another bus for the longest part of the journey. Wearily she settled into a seat by a window.

"I'll have to make up the second Marathi language exam," she thought, "I certainly can't study on this crowded bus any better than I could on the last one. But I'll get practice in listening to Marathi, and maybe speaking a little, so that's not a bad trade."

Not only could she not study on the bus, she found she could not sleep either, particularly if she were to avoid having anything stolen. By the time the bus arrived in Pimpalner she wondered if she would be in any better condition to care for Mrs. Scarf than Bea and Esther were.

Such a rush of passengers when the bus finally stopped at Pimpalner. Carol waited patiently for her turn to exit and then she heard, "There she is!"

Esther's voice carried over the station hubbub. Even in a saree Carol's fair skin made her easy to find in a crowd.

Gratefully, Carol joined the other nurse.

"Isn't that trip something?" Esther asked.

"Yes, I wanted to be able to take right over for you two," she answered.

Esther stepped back to look at her.

"No, we can handle it one more night while you rest up," she said.

"We'll see," she answered; but after a light supper she gratefully accepted their offer and went to bed early. In the morning she would be able to take over.

But in the morning Carol continued to sleep. The two nurses let her rest until the following morning, when Carol assumed their duties.

After 36 hours of sleep, Carol felt able to care for her patient. She sent the two exhausted nurses to bed and immediately began taking Mrs. Scarf's vital signs. Suddenly the elderly missionary's condition became critical. Her pulse faltered, continued weakly, then faltered again.

"You must call Esther and Bea again," Carol told the servant girl.

"But they've just retired," the girl answered.

"I know that, and I hate to arouse them so soon, but I fear Mrs. Scarf is leaving us," Carol explained.

Without a word the girl sped off to call everyone in the household. Soon they all gathered around Mrs. Scarf. In a few moments she peacefully slipped into her wonderful Savior's presence. Carol faced death before, but she felt shock at her passing. This was reality. A missionary might die on the field. Anyone at any age can die of cancer. She herself might die, even as Mrs. Scarf had.

By evening the household settled down again, so the women rested on cots until morning. Carol hoped Esther and Bea would be able at last to sleep, but as soon as they turned out the lights, they heard rats running all around the room.

"Is it always like this?" Carol asked. She couldn't believe she slept through such commotion the last two nights.

"Yes, we are infested with them," Bea replied. "Besides that, they are a real danger because of the plague."

Esther added, "Right across the street the authorities carry out people nearly every day who die from the plague."

Carol knew the fleas on rats sometimes carried bubonic plague but she had not known the plague was actually in the area. Just then a rat jumped onto her cot and ran over her hair.

She screamed and jumped up to get a light.

"They may have already bitten me," she said, "but I'm not going to give them another chance."

Bringing the light to the center of the room, she asked, "What are the authorities doing about it—besides carrying dead people out?"

"You'll find out when you take the bus back to the mission station," Bea explained. "The government is trying to stop the spread of the plague by injecting travelers with serum. Government doctors are the only ones they trust with the serum. They are trying to inoculate people at all public gathering places."

Carol raised her eyebrows as if to ask what she meant.

Esther explained, "You know—like schools and train and bus stations. A bus will not leave without the assurance that everyone on it has been injected."

"But I didn't know Indian doctors had that kind of equipment. We've heard they don't have enough hypodermic needles for these emergencies," Carol interrupted.

"That's the problem," Bea agreed. "They use the same needle for everyone."

"But don't worry. They may let us bring our own needle when you go to the bus," Esther said.

By daylight the three nurses knew they would not sleep, so they got up and helped Carol get ready to return to the station. Carol needed no urging to leave the plague-infested area. After breakfast they gathered the rest of the household together for a few minutes and prayed for the safety of the workers in Pimpalner and for Carol's safety as she traveled. They especially asked the Lord to allow the Indian doctors to use the syringe from the mission clinic so that Carol would not catch some other disease from their contaminated needle.

With all their precautions, Carol was concerned she might have already been infected by a flea during the night. So she trusted not in the injection, but in the Lord. Had He not promised that no evil would befall her and no plague come near her dwelling? She praised the Lord for intervening for her once more as the Indian doctor gladly received the new needle from her. She praised God again as she safely returned to the mission station and her regular duties.

Chapter 12

PARI'S SECRET

"Is it right to kill my husband?"

Pari didn't think it mattered. She loved another man, so the only important thing was to kill Baba quietly, in a way no one would ever guess and no one would ever find out.

Perhaps if she prayed to the neat row of gods lined up in her house, they would help her to succeed. Day after day she dedicated herself to one god or the other, hoping for a foolproof idea. Courage did not come quickly. She discarded plan after plan. After much thought, she finally decided to put tasteless rat poison into Baba's food. That would accomplish the matter most easily.

She waited for a good time to act—others in town were sick with a strange illness, perhaps brought on by the anger of the gods. So Pari cooked a tasty meal of rice and lentils, adding an extra measure of red pepper to conceal any possible taste of the poison.

Baba ate it with relish. What a good cook his wife was! What a lucky man he was to have married her! His stomach full, he settled himself for the night.

"Ohhh! Ohhh! My stomach!"

Baba's groans awakened Pari in the middle of the night. She arose and hurriedly arranged her saree around her. Rushing to his side she hid a smile as she bent over her suffering husband. She must act the part of the concerned and loving wife.

Baba turned to the wall and vomited the black, foul-smelling supper. Pari quickly covered it with dust from the bare floor of their hut. No one must guess! How she hoped her husband would attribute his sudden illness to the strange malady others in the village had experienced. He must not suggest that it had anything to do with her cooking.

Baba's groans increased. Between spasms of pain he tried to talk.

"What is it? How can I help?" Pari asked, kneeling at his side.

"The witch doctor," he gasped, rising on one elbow. "Only the witch doctor will know what to do for this terrible pain."

"Yes," Pari agreed. "Surely his incantations will heal you."

"Go for him," Baba pleaded.

Pari soothed him by saying, "Yes, I will call him—right away in the morning. You know these are the dark nights of the month. I can't go to his village until tomorrow."

Baba lay back to wait for morning. She was right. He could not ask her to venture out in the pitch darkness. He must be content to wait for morning when his good wife would fetch the witch doctor to him. Her promise quieted him. He slept fitfully throughout the rest of the night.

At first light Pari aroused her neighbors to look in on her husband while she ran to the next village to get the witch doctor. In her absence other neighbors came to offer sympathy, and suggestions for treatment. Soon Pari returned. Too weak to rise, Baba heard the jingling of the witch doctor's ankle bracelets and the tinkling of the bells on his ankles, wrists, and three-pronged staff.

Pari continued to play the part of a distressed and loving wife. Before the witch doctor asked how she would pay him, she offered her prized rooster. The witch doctor readily agreed to cast out the evil spirit for the price. The watching neighbors nodded in sympathy and approval.

Inside the small reed and mud hut the witch doctor took command. He quickly bared Baba's stomach and examined him, then lay a large peacock feather, his "degree", on the affected part.

"Very serious," he muttered. "The chant must be long to cure such a one."

Pari agreed and waited with the neighbors while the witchdoctor chanted and danced around his patient. He jingled his bracelets and bells, occasionally shaking his staff toward Baba. Baba continued to moan, periodically drawing up his knees as though in great pain.

Suddenly the witch doctor stopped.

"This one is very bad," he said. "If Pari and Baba will agree, I must use my most drastic method of treatment."

"Yes, of course," Pari agreed.

Baba mumbled something, as he was slipping into a coma. The witch doctor took this as assent. He pulled a special metal rod from a skin of charms and other tools he had dropped at the doorway when he entered. He placed the metal rod in the hot coals of their fire pit. Every moan of his patient increased his speed. When the rod glowed red, he withdrew it from the coals and lightly touched three places across the patient's aching abdomen. The smell of burning flesh filled the hut as Baba screamed and pulled back from the red hot iron. The witch doctor, rising to the occasion, tried to soothe him with another chant.

In a few minutes Baba relaxed again and slipped back into a coma. The witch doctor returned to his charm bag and brought out a small piece of paper covered with curious writings and markings. He put the paper in a metal holder and began another chant, calling on the spirits to bless the charm. Then he tied it around Baba's waist.

From the fire pit Pari brought the witch doctor a cup of tea which he noisily sipped from the saucer. When he finished drinking he told her to give Baba only tea and strained rice water. Then he picked up the prize rooster, which neighbors caught for him, and left.

As the neighbors filed out of her house, Pari overheard them talking to each other. Good! They expected Baba to recover. She welcomed the words of one neighbor who suggested the only reason he might not recover would be if the illness had been caused by the evil eye of the woman across the way. Everyone noted Pari's tender care of her husband.

But Baba failed to respond despite this expensive treatment. Before nightfall he went to the place of the gods.

Throughout the time of the witch doctor's visit, no one noticed Pari and Baba's little girl shrinking into the corner. She cringed as the witch doctor administered the drastic branding of Baba's abdomen. Now that her father was dead, Anuseya mourned as she watched the villagers place his body on the burning bier. In the days that followed she grieved so deeply she didn't notice her mother's attention turning to the one Pari told her to call "Uncle."

In a few weeks Pari married Uncle. She congratulated herself that no one knew of her sin, but she lived in fear that someone might discover her secret.

Although Pari had not loved Baba, she adored their child Anuseya. Shortly after Pari's marriage to Uncle, Anuseya developed a fever, which increased daily and brought with it a cough. When the cough did not go away, Pari became anxious for her child.

"Here, Anuseya. Come and eat the spicy rice I made for you," Pari begged at every meal.

"I cannot," Anuseya would answer. "My heart hurts with yearning for my father, and my stomach is not hungry."

Day by day Pari tried to tempt her with the foods she formerly loved.

"You are getting so thin—I fear for you," Pari said.

Anuseya shook her head and turned away. Maybe it would be good to go to the place of the gods with her father.

Lovingly Pari cradled her like a little child.

"I would not know you were of marriageable age if you were not my own," Pari soothed. "You are no bigger than when you were eight years old and still my little girl. Please eat for me."

Anuseya would try, but the food stuck in her throat, making her cough more.

Pari's good friend Tana lived next door. They lightened their chores by doing them together whenever they could. The two women enjoyed gossiping as they ground their grain or did their washing at the river. Pari shared her concerns about Anuseya with Tana.

One day Tana announced, "There's talk of a new Sadhu in the next village. Perhaps he would have a quick treatment for Anuseya's terrible disease."

"A holy man," Pari mused. "Yes, if there is a cure surely a holy man would have it."

That evening she talked it over with Uncle. The next day she and Anuseya made the trip to talk to this Sadhu and his patients. At once they were encouraged to find a group of sixteen patients who planned to stay for treatment. Pari and Anuseya stayed for several days, but did not take part because they had not paid the sadhu's charge of Rs.300, more than a year's amount of cash. How could they give this enormous sum even if it might be successful?

Each evening they watched as the Sadhu lit a big bon fire and asked his patients to stand around it in a circle. A man began to beat slowly and lightly upon drums as the patients walked in a circle around the fire. The drums beat faster. The patients began to dance. The dancing increased in speed as the drums beat faster and faster. Occasionally they called upon the spirits to come into them and cure them.

Pari watched for hours as they went around and around. The thin, pale faces of the patients reflected the glare of the fire. Some appeared ready to collapse; others rested, even as Anuseya rested at Pari's feet. When the fire finally burned down to a few glowing coals, Anuseya roused herself to listen to the Sadhu's instructions. She watched with her mother as the patients followed him, walking across the fiery coals. He taught them, and they followed—this must be a positive cure! The two watchers agreed, none of the patients' feet were burned. What a miracle!

Pari longed for Anuseya to take part in the treatment. She must try in some way to get Rs.300.

Sadly they returned home. Neither Pari nor Uncle had the Rs.300. They must find another way. Day by day she watched her daughter's increasing weakness and coaxed her to eat.

Tana again brought hopeful news, for she grieved with her friend over her failing daughter.

"Pari, I heard of a place where sick people are treated with loving care. One has told me of hopeless cases that have recovered there," she told her friend one grinding day.

"Another expensive Sadhu?" Pari guessed.

"Even riskier than that," Tana admitted. "But they say it is true."

A glimmer of hope arose in Pari's heart.

"So, where is it?" she asked.

Tana sat back on her heels to watch her friend's reaction.

"The mission clinic," she said, lowering her voice as though it were a dark secret.

"Oh, I don't know," Pari responded. "Those are not our people," she continued.

"I know. But some of them are," Tana observed.

"I'll think about it," Pari stated, ending the conversation.

Instead of going to the clinic, Pari began taking Anuseya to the witch doctor. Day after day, after repeated visits to him, Anuseya worsened. Tana watched and occasionally brought up the subject of the clinic. Pari began asking the advice of other villagers.

Coming back from the village garden, an older woman said, "Yes. Do take Anuseya to the clinic. I have heard much good about them."

But on another day, at the well, several women said, "No! Don't take her there. The spirits will surely become angry. Anuseya will only grow worse."

That afternoon Pari looked at Anuseya and realized if she didn't find treatment soon, she would lose her little Anuseya. She began to think perhaps she was being punished for killing her husband. If so, no amount of treatment by the witch doctor or by anyone else would make Anuseya well. She had not tried the mission clinic, and although it was 23 miles away, she made up her mind to go there.

"Go with us," she begged her husband that evening. "I know only that a white woman there gives out something called medicine, but there is no hope anywhere else."

"Yes," he agreed. "Because I love you and little Anuseya, I will go."

Anuseya could no longer walk, so her uncle carried her the three miles to the bus. At the end of the hot, bumpy and dusty ride he carried her another mile to the Mission clinic.

The white woman (Carol) appeared strange to them, but her smile and obvious concern for Anuseya soon overcame their fear of her. Another kind of fear arose when Carol told them her daughter had the dreaded disease, tuberculosis. Pari had heard that no one recovers from that disease.

An Indian doctor examined Anuseya and prescribed medicine for her. Before Carol gave them the medicine, she and the doctor bowed their heads and prayed for Anuseya. As the three of them got ready to return to the bus, Carol told them, "The medicine is very important. Please do just as the doctor told you. But praying to the living God, 'Jesus,' is the most important of all. He is the one who can heal Anuseya's body. He is the one who can take away your sin."

Pari pondered the missionary's words. She had never heard of Jesus before. While they waited for Anuseya's turn to see the doctor, a missionary told them the story of Jesus.

"Jesus is truly God. Jesus loves you and Anuseya, too. Jesus healed sick people like Anuseya." She remembered the words exactly.

Could the missionary have really talked to Jesus? That is what the missionary lady said. She had asked Jesus to make Anuseya well. Pari wondered if she dared to believe in this foreign god.

Once a week Pari and her husband faithfully carried Anuseya back to the clinic for examination and more medicine. Every time they went they heard more of Jesus' love. Anuseya began to improve week by week.

One week they heard of Jesus' death on the cross for their sins, and Pari was especially impressed. She began to understand that Jesus really is God, that He sees all we do and knows all that is in our hearts. Considering this caused Pari to spend many sleepless nights. Jesus knew she murdered her husband. He might forgive other sins, but could He forgive this one—the killing of another person? Pari learned to say John 3:16, that had the words "Whosoever believeth in Him should not perish but have everlasting life." Faith grew in her heart. The more she heard about Jesus, week by week, the more she trusted in Him. One day she realized she believed Jesus died for her sin, even the sin of murder.

"Oh, God," she confessed, "I know I am the worst sinner in the world. But you died for even my sin and I trust you to be my Savior."

The experience of joy and peace came into her life. Anuseya herself believed during her recovery time. Their lives changed: they no longer went to the witch doctor for healing or for instruction about worshiping evil spirits out of fear.

Soon Anuseya could walk. Once a month she and Pari traveled by foot and by bus to get her supply of medicine. They eagerly looked forward to the time the missionaries would spend with them studying the Bible. Carol enjoyed teaching them and watching them grow in the Lord and in their faith. When Carol was able to visit their village her heart was encouraged by their testimony of bearing a witness to their neighbors.

At the clinic Pari learned to pray and expect God to answer her prayers. She began witnessing to her neighbors and to her husband. Now it was her turn to share good news with Tana about Jesus. Tana saw how

God healed Anuseya, so she willingly sat and listened. In the springtime they talked as they worked together in the fields.

Their plots of seedlings would soon be big enough to transplant into the bigger fields. The whole town met to decide each person's transplanting day. Tana's day came and everyone helped her transplant the seeds during a good rainy spell. Then followed a dry time. The fields needed to be muddy, but there was no sign of the needed rain. The appointed day for Pari's turn was fast approaching but the sky remained clear and blue with not a sign of a cloud.

One morning Pari sat in Tana's house helping her grind some jvari into flour, to make bread for the family. They both looked discouraged, but Pari began to tell Tana that Jesus was the true and living God.

She said, "Those idols on your shelf can't answer prayer, but Jesus can. You should believe in Him."

Then she thought of her own need. There had to be rain in two days or she would miss her turn to plant. The ground was dry and cracked. Here she had told Tana Jesus answers prayer. Did she believe God would send rain—enough to make it muddy to plant her nagali?

Tana did not answer: she just stared at her. When they finished the grinding, Pari went to one side of the room and sat down, bowing her head to the floor. She began to pray aloud, earnestly beseeching the Lord.

"Lord, you said I am like Elijah. He prayed that it would rain, even after it had not rained for three and a half years. Then you sent a big storm and lots of rain. Lord, it hasn't rained for so long. The ground is dry and cracked like in Elijah's time. Send rain now like you sent when he prayed. And Lord send it on time."

Then she remembered God's promise to Elijah, "The effectual, fervent prayer of a righteous man availeth much."

Quietly she left her friend's house and went home to take care of her family. In confidence she went to sleep that night, having cast all her burden upon the Lord. In the night she awoke to the feel of drops of rain falling through her thin grass roof. She lay and listened as it increased and began to pour big drops: musaldar (heavy downpour), as big as her pestle to thresh the rice from its husk. God was answering her prayer, and the next morning all would be well, as the neighbors came to help her plant her field. Her heart filled with praise as she thanked God over and over again for this miracle.

That miracle spoke to Tana and her family as they saw the Lord work for Pari. One by one they also turned to the Lord.

Pari's influence in her village continued. After the forest wood cutters repaired the jungle road so the missionaries could go by jeep, Carol and some others took their tents and lived in Pari's village for a while. Anuseya recovered enough to work and went to live with relatives where she continued to tell people about Jesus. Pari spent each day with Carol. She brought water morning and evening. During the day she took Carol to nearby villages to talk to the women about the Lord Jesus Christ. They walked to all these places because there were no roads even for a jeep. Pari would pull Carol up the steep places and steady her while they walked over the stones and rocks in the streams. When they sat and rested under the trees, they spent the time praying and rejoicing in the Lord. Many women in the Koswan hills put aside their work and listened to the Gospel over and over again. Pari's changed life showed them that the Word of God is the power of God unto salvation to everyone that believes.

In the afternoons, after returning to the tent, Pari would call women from her town for a Bible study. One young married woman who lost two babies came faithfully. One day she stayed after the study time to share her heart with Carol and Pari.

"My life is miserable," she began to cry.

Carol set aside the Bible study materials she had been using and gave all her attention to the young woman.

"I know it must be difficult to live with your husband's family," she began.

"My mother-in-law blames me that our two babies died. She says the fact that they died so soon after they were born proves it is my fault."

Carol began to comfort her, because of her loss, but the woman cut her off.

"That's not the worst," she said. "She has been threatening me since our second baby died, that if we have a third baby, and it does not live, she will send me out of her home. Now I find I have a third child coming."

"We'll pray with you," Carol promised.

"We'll pray for you every day," Pari added.

As the months went on Pari kept her promise, even after Carol had to return to the mission clinic. Carol instructed the young mother in prenatal care. This knowledge and daily prayer greatly encouraged her until the healthy new baby came into their home.

Pari's changed life made a difference in her family and her village.

Chapter 13

BROKEN IDOLS

"The gods blessed us by giving us a new house," Shivram said to his wife Tana. "Now we must have the sadhu come to bless the house itself."

Tana nodded. It would be the only way, for the idols would be angry if they did not dedicate the house to them.

So family and friends gathered. The sadhu came and with great ceremony he blessed the house. Shivram paid a great sum of money so the respected sadhu danced furiously around the house, jingling the bells on his ankles and arms. At each doorway he paused to dance back and forth, shaking his ceremonial spear toward the house. Over the main door he hung a bamboo pole decorated with strings, blessed garlic, bones and teeth. Shivram hoped he was getting his money's worth but whether he did or not, this was the only way to protect himself and his family.

The sadhu and the guests enjoyed a feast with Shivran and Tana after the ceremony. There was much talk of how the gods had blessed Shivran and his family with the lovely new house and how the demons would be turned away by the sadhu's good work.

Hearing the comments of their guests, Tana felt content. However, a few days later Shivram began building a shelf on the wall of the eating area in their new house. She did not need to ask. Her husband was putting up an idol shelf.

"It is such a long shelf," she finally said.

"For all the family gods," he explained. "We must be sure we have not left a single important god out."

Tana watched him hang pictures of several of his favorite idols on the wall above the shelf. How can we be sure we have not left out a god? Tana wondered. There were hundreds of gods. How could they know which were the important gods?

"Now, we must burn incense to them," Shivram instructed.

Shivram placed the burning incense then he and Tana bowed before the idol shelf, anxious to do anything to insure a safe and happy home. He concluded their first family idol worship in the new house by commenting, "Surely now the evil spirits will leave us alone. We will enjoy good health and successful farming." Tana hoped he was right.

In spite of their expense and efforts, the gods did not bless them. Soon after the dedication, Shivram stepped on a poison thorn. Tana bound up her husband's sore foot. At first she did not worry about the misfortune.

"Surely the idols are pleased with our offerings. They will make your foot well, quickly," she consoled.

Faithfully Shivram and Tana burned incense and expected his foot to heal, but instead it became infected. Before long Shivram had difficulty walking on it. They began to question whether they should call the sadhu again. Yet surely the recent house blessing should take care of the problem.

One afternoon Tana returned from the market to report that the missionary evangelistic team had come to the village.

"Pari says they have a doctor with them," she said. "I told her I didn't know if you would want to go to the missionary doctor...."

Shivram interrupted. "I am so frustrated. Surely the house offering was not big enough. Why else would the god send this demon to live in my foot?"

Tana soothed, "I do not understand these things, either. The idols have not helped. Maybe the missionaries can."

The next day Shivram went to the missionaries for treatment. While he waited for his turn he heard the way of salvation for the first time. That evening he felt some relief from the infection so the next day he eagerly returned for more medicine. Day by day he kept going back to the missionaries. He listened more eagerly each time. He realized his heart's need was greater than his foot's need.

Tana did most of the farming until his foot improved, but in the evenings he told her what he learned. Pari had been witnessing to Tana, so she knew a little about what he learned at the clinic.

"I am confused," he admitted one evening. "I fear the demons, of course, even as we have been taught as children."

"But the fear of them makes us search always for peace," Tana agreed.

Shivram nodded. "Can you imagine a god of love?" he asked.

"Pari says the Lord Jesus Christ is such a god," Tana answered. "She says he loves us and died for us."

"Our idols expect our fear; they might want us to die for them," Shivram went on. "But I cannot imagine a god dying for a man."

"And if he is a god, he became the sacrifice for our sin," Tana added. "At least that's what Pari says."

"Did she tell you he arose from the dead?" Shivram asked. "If it is all true, that would surely prove his sacrifice was accepted. I am not sure I can believe all this."

The next evening Shivram reflected out loud on the many times he went to the big fair and festival at Saptrasingh.

"Always I offer a goat to the brightly painted eighteen-foot-high goddess. But every time I come home feeling depressed and futile."

"I did not know," Tana murmured. She was surprised to learn how depressed the festival made him feel.

"Because the goddess never shows in any way if she accepts my offering or if she will bless us."

Tana's eyes widened in wonder.

"The goddess has eighteen hands," she reminded him. "Surely she has enough to bless us all."

Shivram did not feel free to share all his heart with Tana. At night, instead of sleeping, he pondered what he was learning about the Lord Jesus Christ. What would it mean to take the step of believing in this new God?

Day after day, as the Indian evangelist taught from his book called the Bible, faith began to grow in Shivram's heart. At night he and Tana continued to discuss whether Jesus Christ really was God—the true and living God. On the days that Tana did not have to be in the fields, she went to the clinic with her husband. The missionary taught her the same things Shivram had been learning. Sometimes she came with Pari, Anuseya, and other women of the village to the tent where Carol stayed.

None of them could read but Tana faithfully carried her New Testament.

Their children learned to read at a Hindu school. On special holidays the children came home. Shivram and Tana were grateful they had a New Testament available for them. Each day of the children's vacations the family gathered to read God's Word.

After the missionaries left the village Pari went to work in Shivram and Tana's home and fields. Then came the time of testing, to see if Pari's God really did answer prayer.

The evening after Pari prayed for rain at Tana's house, Tana shared her thoughts with Shivram.

"If Pari's God answers and does the impossible, I will know for sure He is the living and true God."

"But Pari's planting time is in two days," Shivram reminded her. "Rain never comes without two or three days of gathering clouds and there is not a cloud in the sky. It really would be a miracle," he laughed.

Tana and Shivram awoke to the sound of the downpour in the middle of the night. They got up and looked outside, almost afraid to express the wonder they felt.

Finally Shivram said, "It must be true. The God of heaven cares about Pari. He heard and answered her prayer."

Tana added, "Surely He is the true and living God, and we too believe in Him."

She glanced at her husband to see if he agreed. Shivram remained in deep thought.

"It does not matter what our relatives say and do, we will be baptized to show everyone we believe. We will pray to the same God Pari does. Truly He is living and He works miracles," he finally said.

From then on Shivram and Tana neglected the old idols. They no longer burned incense, nor put flower garlands over the idols. The fear departed. Instead, joy and peace reigned in their home. When their children Chintman (age 10) and Raja (age 5), came home for a holiday, they found changed parents. Because their parents wanted them to read them the New Testament, they too heard the truth and accepted Christ as Savior.

Two other sons, Ramdas and Sita, came from the ashram (Hindu school dormitories) where they took part in the worship days called Ganpatti. Before coming home they gave money so the teachers could buy a lifesize image of Ganesh, the elephant god. They helped make decorations and garlands then watched boys and girls dancing before the idol.

When they came home they were amazed that their parents did not burn incense nor make offerings to Ganesh on their home idol shelf. They too read the New Testament and learned about the Lord Jesus Christ, the true and living God. This was not new to them, for they heard many songs about Jesus, coming from the Christian church and mission dormitories near the Hindu school. They shared with their parents how they sneaked through the fence to sit in on the Christian meetings on Sundays. They would have been scolded, punished or maybe confined to the compound if they had been caught by their teachers.

When Ramdas and Sita returned to the dormitories, they were required to take part in morning and evening chants to the idols. Before they considered it a normal part of Indian life. Now they wanted no part of it. They learned to pray to Jesus instead of worshiping idols. Faith began to grow in Ramda's and Sita's hearts too as they heard more about Jesus when the family gathered to read God's Word. They suffered for refusing to take part in the chants. Soon they had to look for other schooling.

Not long after the family's conversion, the annual four-day women's Bible class met in Kalvan. Tana arrived early with Chintman and Sadam, and the three of them listened and grew in the Lord. Chintman sat next to the teacher and read all the Scriptures the teacher referred to in her lessons. Carol's heart thrilled to see the growth in the lives of these new Christians.

The next time the evangelistic tour came to their village, Pari met them when they arrived.

She said, "Shivram and Tana are calling you to their home. They have been saved. Now they want to be baptized to show others they believe in the Lord Jesus Christ. They want to be fully dedicated to Him."

The following morning, normal village scenes greeted the missionaries on the way to Shivram's house. Children let goats and cattle out of the houses, where they had been tied all night. Herd boys gathered cattle to take to the mountains to graze. A man sat on a stone slab, bathing himself with a pail of water and a stone, in place of soap.

Tana paced the floor waiting for the missionaries to come. When they arrived she welcomed them into their house.

"Come in," she said, throwing open the door and bowing respectfully.

She spread two throw rugs on the floor. The women gathered on one rug and the men on the other. As they sat, Carol noticed the idols on the shelf, but they evidently had not been worshiped for some time. No incense burned and the flower garlands were all dried.

Tana served them hot tea by turns. She didn't have enough cups to serve them all at one time. The men made plans for the baptism, carefully discussing Shivram's understanding of the Gospel and of the step he and his family wanted to take. Vijay, the evangelist, gradually brought up the subject of the idols.

"And do you still believe in the idols and worship the evil spirits?" he asked.

Shivram quickly replied, "I never worship them any more. I believe that Jesus is God—the true and living God."

Shivram then rose from his place on the rug, took down all the idols, the pictures of the idols, and the bamboo pole that had been placed over the entry way to drive off the evil spirits. Then he left the house for a long period of time. The guests did not speculate on what he was doing, but talked generally about the changes that come into a Christian's life.

When Shivram came back into the house he said, "I have broken my idols. I have destroyed my idols. I no longer fear them. I believe in the Lord Jesus Christ. My wife and my children do too. We want to follow the Lord all the way. We want to be baptized."

At the close of the week of Bible teaching, Vijay baptized Shivram and his family. Not all the family and friends that had been to the house dedication came to the baptism, but all of them heard about it. Tana remembered thinking how satisfied she had felt at their neighbors' comments about the dedication. Now she did not care what other people said. She wanted to please the true and living God, Jesus Christ.

Shortly after the baptism, Ramdas enrolled in a Christian school. After two years of daily Bible teaching, he also accepted Christ as his Savior. He later married a Christian girl and moved home to help his parents farm.

Sita stayed in the Hindu ashram another year to finish high school. Because she loved the Lord, she refused to take part in the Hindu idol worship. God used that to strengthen her faith. After finishing high school she attended Bible college for a year to become better grounded in the faith.

Ramdas and Sita were married on the same day. Sita and her Christian husband moved to a far away town where they could share their faith with another group of Kokani tribespeople. Many of them have come to Christ.

Sunday School children by their home

Mrs. Gaikwad and Yamona Gavit—teachers
at Ladies Bible Conference in Kalvan

Making furniture for Carol

Chapter 14

THE SUDDEN RAINSTORM THAT NEVER CAME

The evangelistic team approached Desgaon in their usual manner: prayerfully and carefully. They entered the small village early in the morning and set up for an evangelistic meeting. Vijay played the accordion and the rest of the team sang along with him. The happy music attracted a crowd of villagers who stayed to listen to what this strange mixture of foreign missionaries and native preachers had to say. Vijay and Jayant took turns sharing the Gospel message.

Carol sat with the women, encouraging them to listen and discouraging them from leaving to do their house work. All during the meeting her heart continued to pray for the preacher and the listeners.

After the meeting the team broke up into pairs to visit in the village homes. Carol and her helper talked to the women. A group of women gathered in the part of the village where they were. Carol took the opportunity to explain the Gospel of the Lord Jesus Christ.

She noticed something unusual. An old man named Chindya sat near the crowd of women. When the group broke up, the Bible ladies began visiting in homes again. He followed to three or four homes.

Curious, Carol asked him, "Have you heard of the true and living God?"

"Yes," he answered. "My son has been over the mountain to the next district. He brought back a Bible."

Their hearts were encouraged. Maybe Chindya would be a good contact in Desgaon.

On their next visit to Desgaon Chindya again joined the group of listeners. After the Bible teaching he asked, "Big Sister, would you come and teach us next Sunday? Could your group come every Sunday morning?"

The evangelistic team gladly made weekly visits to share the Gospel, meeting in Chindya's house. During the visitation time, after each group meeting, Carol or one of the other missionaries met with Chindya. They tried to teach him the truth of the Gospel. After several weeks they became discouraged. He insisted on mixing Hindu spiritism with the teachings of the Bible. Gradually, he showed less interest in having the group come on Sundays.

One Sunday Chindya's sister, from the neighboring village of Khadakvan, visited in his home. She attended the small group meeting, listening carefully to the ladies who talked with her afterward.

"I would like to learn more," she said. "Could you come to our village too?"

The team prayerfully considered her request. The next week they went to Khadakvan instead of Desgaon. By the end of the dry season a large group of villagers regularly gathered in Khadakvan to hear God's Word.

Rainy season isolates the villages from the evangelistic teams, but the next October the team returned to Khadakvan. A dry spell promised relatively passable roads to the villages. Team members piled into the jeep with New Testaments, Gospel portions, and tracts. The team sang choruses in the Marathi language along the way making the ten mile journey over ruts and around remaining mud holes seem shorter.

Not far from the mission station the jeep overtook a common road hazard. A tractor took up so much road room they could not pass. Tractors were scarce in that part of India. The farmer proudly drove it down the middle of the road where anyone who came along could envy his prosperity.

"Hey, move that thing," one of the jeep occupants yelled. The rest of them joined in.

The tractor driver didn't turn his head. His noisy machine blocked out all other sounds.

Carol honked the horn. Everyone shouted. Still no response. The team members looked at each other and laughed.

Jayant suggested, "Stop. I will get out of the jeep and run up even with the tractor to get the farmer's attention."

Carol stopped the jeep. Jayant got out and ran ahead, waving to get the farmer's attention. Everyone laughed as the farmer timidly looked around. He pulled to the side of the road then watched the evangelist climb into the jeep. The team waved and began singing again as they drove away.

Carol parked the jeep at the edge of a narrow part of Lake Chandkapur. The only way to Khadakvan was across a single width footbridge. Each team member picked up literature or equipment he was responsible for and began the mile walk. A welcoming committee met them as they reached the village. The villagers remembered their promise to return after the rainy season.

Kamelbai invited the group into her home then spread a rug for them to sit on. Tulshiram called the neighbors for a Bible class. While they waited for the crowd to gather, the villagers joined in singing Gospel choruses and hymns they learned the year before. The hearty singing showed their eagerness to hear again of Jesus Christ the true and living God.

As Jayant began the Bible lesson, Carol looked around Kamelbai's main room. Every wall showed evidence of evil spirit worship that had held Kamelbai's family in fear all their lives. Chalk drawings on the inside walls and charms hung here were designed to keep away the evil ones. Carol knew once a year the people of Khadakvan formed a group to travel from village to village collecting an offering to appease an evil spirit. The native preachers told her how the villagers danced in front of homes then waited for an offering of money, rice, flour or anything of value. They went from village to village until they decided they had enough money to purchase a small goat for the blood offering.

Carol remembered observing part of their ritual. They took the goat to the top of the mountain where they offered its blood and left the tail. Taking the rest of the goat down to their village, they cooked a big dinner for all to share. They drank, danced and called on the evil spirits. Some of the group became possessed with demons. Carol shuddered. She remembered seeing a villager pushing a demon possessed man around in a circle with the man bent back so far she couldn't understand why he didn't fall to the ground.

Bringing her mind back to the present, she prayed silently for the people gathered there, hoping they would understand the Gospel Jayant explained.

"The true and living God does not want an offering of goat's blood," he proclaimed.

Their empty faces showed they did not understand that God's Son, the Lord Jesus Christ, gave His blood on the cross once for all.

Jayant continued.

"Jesus died on the cross for you; for me. He was buried in a nearby grave, but triumphantly rose again on the third day."

After the group meeting, Carol met with the women. She explained the Gospel several times, trying to make it plain. In the smaller group, the listeners began to discuss what they heard.

"This is wonderful news," one woman said.

Another quietly confessed, "I do believe. I want to follow Jesus as my God."

Other women nodded their heads. They, too, believed.

The beginning of another season of serving the Lord in this village had been profitable. Just as the team gathered their things together to start the walk back to the jeep, a villager rushed in shouting, "Big Sister, don't go now. A big rain storm is headed our way. It will soon reach the lake and come across to our village. Wait until it is over."

Carol visualized walking through mud in her sandals and walking right out of them as the mud claimed them with a "slurp." She joined the group that went out to look at the dark cloud. It was coming toward Khadakvan. From their vantage point they could see it reach the opposite shore of Lake Chandkapur. Sheets of water poured from the clouds, striking the waves below.

Carol remembered how Elijah prayed it would not rain for three and a half years. She had told the villagers that Jesus was a powerful God who stilled storms and quieted the waves. They had heard about God answering prayer. Now it was time to pray.

They all bowed their heads to talk to the heavenly Father. Carol prayed, "Father, we thank you that the whole world is in your hand. You stopped the rain in the time of Elijah. We believe you can do the same today."

When they finished praying Carol said to the quiet crowd, "It isn't hard for the Lord to tip His hand and the rainstorm will change directions."

Every person looked toward the lake and the approaching storm. God did exactly what Carol had said. The storm turned a complete 90 degree angle to the north, leaving a dry path to the foot bridge.

That day God showed the people of Khadakvan He is truly powerful. The evangelistic team walked across the dry footbridge to the jeep and settled themselves for the return trip. They drove no more than twenty feet before they had to ford streams of water running across the road.

Soon after that, Jayant baptized over 25 people who openly professed the Lord. Believers began gathering each morning to sing and pray before going to work. They did the same in the evening when they returned. Although most of the villagers could not read, their children read the Scriptures to them when they came home from boarding school on vacations and weekends. Because of God's mighty power, a thriving congregation of believers continues to worship together in the village of Khadakvan.

Chapter 15

TANABAI AND HER TRIALS

"Jayant, are you and Vijay ready to leave tomorrow morning for our week in Verula?" Carol asked as she looked up from her check list of equipment.

"We will be ready by the time you need to load the jeep," he smiled. Then he added, "Let me help you gather the big pieces."

Together they gathered and checked off four tents, a folding table, chairs, cots, Carol's burshane (propane) tank and stove, the film projector, films, the accordion, boxes of literature, and space for ten suitcases. As usual, they would need to make two jeep-and-trailer trips to the chosen village.

After an early breakfast the next morning, Carol supervised the stowing of equipment into the trailer, checking off the first load. She double checked the cans of gasoline that would enable them to make daily evangelistic visits to nearby villages. All the luggage was loaded, then the evangelistic group gathered in a circle. Vijay led them in prayer before they piled into the jeep.

Many miles of driving over Indian jeep tracks and cart ruts had made Carol grateful for the fifteen miles of relatively good road on this trip. When the chatter of getting settled died down, the group began singing Marathi Gospel choruses, which they continued for the first twelve miles. The midmorning sun illuminated the small villages and fields as the jeep progressed up and down, over hills and down across streams.

They came to a steep descent then a short level stretch where a stream ran across the road. There was no bridge, but the jeep forded streams easily. The mechanic who serviced the jeep had declared it in good running order the week before, so Carol was surprised when it stalled. The jeep reached the foot of the descent and the engine stopped. Carol tried several times but the engine would not restart. The singing stopped. Each team member thought, "Will the jeep need to be repaired? We are fifty-five miles from the nearest garage."

Carol climbed out of the jeep, lifted the hood, and peered at the motor. Nothing looked out of the ordinary. She closed her eyes and prayed, "Thank you Lord for bringing us this far. I am trusting you to take us the rest of the way."

As she lifted her head she saw a young friend, Laxman, running down the hill toward the stalled jeep.

Laxman called, "My father and two brothers are in the field at the hilltop and will come to help you."

The team members climbed out of the jeep. The men unhooked the luggage trailer and pulled it to the side of the road. Carol got back behind the wheel when Laxman's father and brothers came. They helped the team men push the jeep the few level feet toward the stream. Suddenly the motor came to life.

"What an answer to prayer!" Carol exclaimed. The men rehooked the luggage trailer and the team climbed back into the jeep. Carol thanked Laxman's father and brothers, then, taking no chances, she put the jeep into four-wheel drive and they safely ascended the hill.

The rest of the trip presented the normal Indian road problems of picking the best route between or over the rocks and ruts. As they came through the last rocky ditch a group of children and young folks from Verula met them. All of them shouted at the same time. The evangelists rejoiced to hear them begging, "Please stay in our village. We will show you a tree where you can pitch your tents."

Carol enjoyed her ministry with these youngsters. Every evening about five o'clock the children returned to the village from their work of grazing the cattle. They gathered in Carol's tent to sing and hear a Bible story. The evening meeting was held in the center of town. After the town meeting, the young people returned to Carol's tent to sing until eleven p.m. This made a long day for Carol as she arose early each morning for her time of devotions with the Lord. The joy of seeing young people respond to the Word of God more than balanced any weariness the schedule brought.

Each afternoon Carol and Mathura visited from house to house, telling of the Lord Jesus Christ, and explaining the Gospel in simple words the villagers could understand. One day she realized the women thought she was saying "Vishnu" when she said "Jesus." Vishnu is the name of one of the Hindu gods.

"No, not Vishnu; Jesus," she said. "Say Jesus."

"Jesus," the women answered.

"Again, Jesus," Carol prompted. "Jesus is the true and living God."

"Jesus," they repeated.

After that she listened to the women to be sure they understood who she was teaching about.

More alert to their reasoning, she listened carefully as they talked about Christ. Sure enough, the same problem occurred when she said "Christ." They thought she was saying "Krishna," the name of another Hindu deity.

"Christ. Jesus Christ, the Son of the only true God," Carol explained.

"Christ; Jesus Christ," they learned to answer.

Without the explanation, no wonder they become confused and want to mix in all their idolatry, Carol thought.

In their schedule of visiting, they came to Tanabai's house on the edge of the village. Tanabai welcomed them eagerly, for she knew Carol from the clinic in Kalvan where Carol had treated her for tuberculosis. Tanabai was the mother of Laxman, and it was her husband Dhanji and her two older sons who had helped the team get the jeep started.

Tanabai saw Carol and Mathura coming to her house. She hurried to the door, calling out, "Welcome! Welcome, dear friend."

She quickly spread a rug for Carol and Mathura to sit. Her two daughters-in-law came out to meet them and joined them on the rug, as did her youngest son and daughter.

Then, as she offered them tea, Tanabai kept up a ceaseless chatter, telling Mathura and her own family all about her visits to the clinic and how much better she felt. She asked about the health of other clinic workers she knew.

After the time of refreshment and catching up on the news, Carol read the Word to Tanabai. She and her family listened intently. Since her visits to the clinic she began to believe in her heart that Jesus was the true God and Savior.

Tanabai's whole family came to the evening evangelistic meetings, except Laxman. It was his duty to stay in the field, day and night, to watch their grain crops. Crows came by day to pluck the grain and thieves by night. Bebi, the small sister at home, took Laxman's meals and water so he did not have to come to the house.

But Laxman was unhappy because he didn't get to come to the meetings. Carol sent a New Testament with Bebi to the field for him. He spent hours reading it.

God's Word is powerful, as it says in Romans 1:16: "I am not ashamed of the Gospel for it is the power of God unto salvation to everyone that believeth." Laxman was born again as he read the Word of God and God opened his heart. One by one his married brothers, their wives, Bebi, and the little brother Hiraman also believed. What a joyous day it was when, last of all, the father Dhanji also put his faith in Jesus Christ.

After two years of regularly visiting in Verula, evangelist Jayant moved his family there. Tanabai and Dhanji offered their home for a house church. Between forty and sixty villagers began regularly attending. Most of those coming did not trust Christ for salvation until Jayant faithfully preached the Word for many months. God used many trials in Tanabai's family to show other villagers His faithfulness.

God's testings perfect every believer who steps out openly for Him. Tanabai and Dhanji had their share of sorrows, beginning with Laxman's health.

Laxman was baptized at the same time as Madhu and Vishwas. His name was changed to Samuel at that time. Shortly thereafter the three of them, with Madhu's sister Anuseya, went to Bible college. While he attended Bible college, Samuel became ill with leukemia, but the Lord gave him the strength to complete three years of Bible college.

After graduating, Vishwas married Anuseya. He and Madhu became evangelists. Samuel, although still suffering with leukemia, served the Lord as assistant house father in the Kalvan Boys' Boarding School. The treatment at Tata Hospital in Bombay arrested the disease for a few years. But later it returned. He also contracted tuberculosis.

Samuel's fellow workers spent much time in prayer for Him. God worked a miracle. The tuberculosis was cured. Samuel still had to go to Bombay once a month for treatment for the leukemia. God still has a special task for Samuel. He gave him a faithful wife to stand by him through their trials, enabling him to serve the Lord as long as he had strength. Tanabai realized God has been faithful to her also in upholding her son.

These testings seemed more than enough, but God was still perfecting Tanabai's family to show forth the Lord's glory. The happy day came when Gunaji (Samuel's brother) and Dhondi had a baby boy.

Yet joy mixed with sorrow when Tanabai discovered both his feet and hands were clubbed, making him disabled. Again God enabled the family to patiently endure the trial, presenting a great testimony of God's faithfulness to their village. This fruit will be seen as others come to know the God of Tanabai and Dhanji.

Chapter 16

THE WITCH DOCTOR AND THE BOIL

"Look! There is the witch's house and she is standing in the doorway." Carol looked in the direction Manda motioned, then at Manda, whose fright-filled eyes locked onto the witch's mesmerizing stare.

Carol grabbed Manda's arm and said, "Let's go down this other path." The witch's shrill voice rang out, "Come to my house. I want to talk to you about something."

Carol quickly whispered, "Manda, be sure you tell me about the witch before we go to her house."

Manda called to the witch, "We will be there in about 20 minutes, after a stop at Dhanibai's house. We promised to see her sick baby."

Carol and Manda stood before Dhanibai's door and cleared their throats. Dhanibai quickly came to the door with a crying baby in her arms. Her smile did not erase the worry lines around her eyes as she sadly related her concerns about the baby's high fever.

Carol retrieved a stethoscope from her bag and held it on the baby's chest. She noticed the runny eyes and nose and the rash on his tiny body. Another case of measles. There were many in Verula. After giving Dhanibai medicines and instruction to care for the little one, both Manda and Carol prayed to the Lord Jesus for the baby's fever to go down, and for Dhanibai's comfort and encouragement. Then Dhanibai prayed, thanking the Lord for bringing help in answer to her prayer.

Yes, Dhanibai was a believer and the only mother in the village who was saved, and teaching her children about Jesus.

While they still sat on Dhanibai's rug, Carol asked, "Manda, now tell me about the witch."

So Manda told her what she knew.

"She has been a witch for many years. She keeps many articles of witchcraft in her house, claiming through her mumblings of mantras that she can do miracles. She is teaching Seilabai across the path from her. Now the demons have been bothering Seilabai, torturing her at night, pulling her hair until the scalp swells into big red welts. They even bite her on her arms."

As Manda described the painful welts and bites, tears came to Carol's eyes. Manda could tell she was praying in her heart for this dear woman.

Manda continued. "Seilabai is frightened. She hung a piece of bamboo over the doorway of her house, hoping the demons will be deceived into entering the bamboo instead of coming into her house."

Carol and Manda, who had been sitting cross-legged on the floor talking to Dhanibai, stood up, saying, "We will come again in the afternoon
to see your baby."

With a prayer in their hearts they hurried down the path to the witch's
house and climbed the steps to the door. There they stood and cleared
their throats, shuffled their feet and finally called out, "Bai!" (Woman!)
The witch appeared from the back of her home. They could barely see
anything through the narrow doorway for the house had no windows to
bring in sunlight. The witch led them into her sitting room. Her voice
sounded foreboding as she offered, "Here; sit on this rug on the floor."

Carol and Manda slowly lowered themselves in the customary cross-
legged position, as they scanned the dimly lit room. A rope bed was
turned on its side with a dirty, ragged, thin quilt thrown over one leg. Just
then two little mice ran back and forth near the wall behind the bed.
Carol hoped the mice wouldn't run around the wall to where the women
were sitting. She shivered as she imagined them running up her back.

"So you are staying in our village?" the witch asked.

Smiling nervously and trying to calm the quaver in her voice, Carol
answered, "Yes, we are living a week in your village. We pitched our
tents under the big tree in the plowed field."

Just then a tall and graceful teen age girl entered the sitting room
from the kitchen. She wiped her hands on one end of her saree, smiled at
them, and said, "I have finished my cooking."

Then she turned to her grandmother, the witch, and asked, "May I sit
for a while? I have brought the water and all is ready for the lunches to
be taken to the men in the field."

The witch nodded her head from side to side, meaning "yes." Jayda sat
down directly in front of Carol and Manda.

She said, "Tell me about the book that tells about God. Have you
brought it with you?"

Carol removed her Bible from her bag and answered, "Jesus is God's
Son. This Book tells about the wonderful miracles He has done."

The witch moved closer, anxious to hear every word Carol said. Carol
told them the story of Jesus raising Jairus' daughter from the dead to
show God's great strength.

Jayda exclaimed, "That is wonderful power!"

The witch nodded, but muttered under her breath, "That was great
but Jesus must have deceived people. My gods can do miracles too. They
can cause some folks to have power to walk over the top of water and not
sink. They can curse people and make them die."

Carol explained the Gospel then she and Manda left with a deep burden to pray for a miracle—for the witch to understand the Gospel and Jayda to understand the truth of the Gospel and not be deceived by her grandmother. Every day that week they stopped to share the Gospel at the witch's house.

On one of those days Jayda asked, "Where did I come from? Why was I born?"

Manda answered, "Do you want to hear about the creation of the world?"

Jayda drew closer and begged, "Tell me all about it."

Manda and Carol told the story of how God created the world and how sin defiled it. Carol explained again how God's Son, the promised Redeemer, gave His life to save fallen man. Jayda nodded her head from time to time.

The week passed with the daily visits and daily telling of sin, punishment for sin, and Jesus' death and resurrection. Even though the witch and Jayda heard of their need to believe in Jesus and trust Him to save their souls, by the end of the week they showed no evidence of faith in their hearts.

Carol returned to her house in Kalvan and Manda to hers in Verula. Before long the monsoon rains came, making roads impassable for cars or jeeps. One day, during the storms, Manda appeared at Carol's house. Carol wondered what important news Manda had to share that would bring her so far through the rain and mud. Manda's red, swollen eyes and downcast expression alerted Carol to trouble.

Carol brought her a jug of water and helped her wash her feet before she drew her into the house.

With no preliminaries, Manda announced, "Jayda is dead."

Carol put her arms around Manda as she explained what happened. "The witch is growing old and she must pass her powers on to someone else, along with the witchcraft fetishes."

Carol nodded. She knew about the magic stones and feathers, pieces of bones and other articles such as the precious items that are wrapped in leather and sewed onto a string to tie around peoples necks. She waited quietly for Manda to continue.

"The grandmother chose Jayda to succeed her but, to really inherit this great power, Jayda had to curse five people and cause their deaths within a certain period of time. If she failed to do this she herself would die. Jayda tried. She really tried. But at the end of the allotted time she could only account for two deaths."

Manda began to weep. Carol hugged her until she regained control of herself. Then Manda went on with her story.

"Yes, sure enough, Jayda became ill with a high fever," she said. "Her left arm swelled to twice its usual size and developed a huge, hard, red spot."

Carol pictured the ugly red boil that must have appeared on Jayda's arm. The pain it caused would have been terrible.

Again Manda stopped to control her tears.

After a few minutes she went on.

"Jayda cried out in severe pain and fright, 'Grandma, have mercy on me and remove the curse.' Her grandmother silently shook her head. One day a whitish yellow spot appeared in the center of the red boil. During the night it burst open. Pus came out but the pain and fever remained."

Manda broke down. Carol wept quietly beside her, hugging her until she was able to resume the story.

"By then Jayda was almost unconscious but she whispered to her grandmother, 'We should have listened to Carol and Manda, believing in their God. Now it is too late—too late—too late.'

"The witch closed Jayda's eyes and screamed, pounding her own head on the floor."

Manda and Carol cried together for several minutes, picturing the great sorrow of Jayda and her grandmother.

Carol opened her Bible and read, Matthew 16:24-26: "Then Jesus said unto His disciples, 'If any man will come after me, let him deny himself, and take up his cross and follow me. For whosoever will save his life shall lose it and whosoever will lose his life for my sake shall find it, for what is a man profited if he shall gain the whole world and lose his own soul? Or what shall a man give in exchange for his soul?'"

Yes, the witch's gods had power, but only the true and living God has power to save.

Chapter 17

DATTU FORSAKES IDOLS TO FOLLOW THE LORD JESUS

"Come another time."

"I am going for water."

"I have to cook."

"I am on the way to the field."

Such were the excuses the women in the villages gave when Carol and her teammates first invited them to evangelistic meetings. Especially in Kalvan, the nurses recognized the need to offer more medical help in order to interest the women. Even then, the villagers treated the evangelistic teams with coldness.

Carol prayed much about the apathy of the villagers. As she did the Lord reminded her of the many times she had heard village parents say, "We would like to send our boys to a boarding school in Kalvan because the village schools only go to the 4th grade."

Carol's daily Bible reading took her to Isaiah 54:13: "And all thy children shall be taught of the LORD and great shall be the peace of thy children."

Then she turned the page back to Isaiah 54:2, "Enlarge the place of thy tent, and let them stretch forth the curtains of thine habitations; spare not, lengthen thy cords, and strengthen thy stakes."

From these verses God led her to open a boys' boarding school in Kalvan.

It is TEAM's policy that, at the beginning of a new work, the missionary who feels led to start a ministry, by faith and prayer should trust the Lord for funds to get it started. However, the Lord prepared the way for this project. Carol had funds set aside. Mrs. Connie Lambert, a friend from her Bible institute days in Phoenix, had designated gifts for Carol's use in the Lord's work. The money was kept in a special fund which Carol used to supply the boys' needs for the first three years.

After consultation with the Indian Field Council, along with continual prayer, plans took shape to open Kalvan Christian Boys' Boarding School. Carol talked with her house boy about the need for more room. He willingly gave up his large bedroom for a smaller room. The large room would sleep eleven boys and a house father. Sakaram Naik agreed to become the house father.

Carol then found an Indian lady in a neighboring village who agreed to come in daily to cook.

News of the new boarding school spread by word of mouth to villagers in the Kalvan area. Parents began bringing their boys, hoping there would be a place for them to stay. Among the boys was one named Dattu. He and his parents came to Carol's house to discuss his schooling. After polite conversation Dattu's father said, "We have one request."

Carol asked, "What is that?"

"When the children are served food would you please serve Dattu first each time?"

Carol answered, "This will not be possible, because we feel all should be treated alike." The conversation turned back to other aspects of the boys' education. When it came time for the parents to decide whether or not to send Dattu to the boarding school his parents realized Dattu's education was more important than his receiving special treatment. However, they felt Carol should know why they had made such a request.

"Dattu is a special boy," his father explained. "For many years after we married we had no children. Finally we went to a temple thirty miles from home. We worshiped the god whose temple is in Satvaichivada and brought offerings of great value to the idol and the holy man who lives there. Because of this sacrifice the god of that temple gave us our one and only child, Dattu."

That explained why Dattu was so special to them. Carol hoped their misplaced faith would not hinder Dattu's reception of the Gospel.

Dattu moved into the boarding school. As required of all the boys, he attended the daily Bible lesson time and memorized the assigned Scripture. More importantly, he took God's Word into his heart. In a short time he placed his faith in the Lord Jesus Christ. His life showed the reality of his belief in Jesus. From then on he kept his New Testament close at hand, either with him or next to his pillow.

Several months later Dattu's parents came with another request.

Again they met Carol in her sitting room. After the polite initial conversation, Dattu's father asked, "We would like permission to take Dattu out of school for a few days so that he may accompany us on our annual trip to the temple in Satvaichivada. Each year we take a gratitude offering for sending us a fine son."

Silently Carol prayed for wisdom to give the right answer. She could not refuse to let them take their own son but neither could she tell them, "Of course, take your son on this trip."

The Lord led her to say, "Let us call Dattu to see what he has to say."

As soon as Dattu heard his parents' request, he said, "Mother, Dad, I don't want to go because I no longer believe in that idol. I believe that Jesus is God's Son. We no longer need to take an offering to that idol. Jesus gave Himself as an offering on the cross, taking our sins and paying the penalty."

The parents' pleas could not change Dattu's resolve to follow the Lord.

Dattu continued through 27 years of walking in his faith, still keeping his New Testament near his pillow. He is a faithful leader in the group of believers in his village of Khadki where he enjoys sharing the work with others from the same village: Devram (another leader), Jayaram, Popat Shaivji, Somaji and others. Most of these men were also in the first group of boys that stayed in Kalvan Boys' Boarding School.

The boys received their academic subjects in a school next to the mission compound. Carol taught Bible to the boys, eventually sharing the duty with Helen Penner, when Helen finished language study. One teaching method was for the boys to gather on rugs laid out on the sand in the yard. There they memorized Bible verses together.

During Carol's furlough of 1965-1966 the Lord used the same donor in Phoenix, plus some others, to supply the need for constructing a larger building. Walter Engblom supervised the erecting of the hostel to house 75 boys. At completion of the building, Carol had the privilege of cutting the ribbon at the dedication ceremony. Through the years God used that building and the servants He placed there to work in the hearts of many boys. The boys' boarding school made a tremendous difference in the villages. Homes opened up and women had time to sit and listen to the teaching of God's Word—no more excuses! Many Indian boys heard the Word of God both mornings and evenings.

Because of the teaching received there, many young men are able to read the Word of God, Bibles are found and used in many homes in the Kalvan area, and Christians are seeking God's way.

Carol and her Jeep

Chapter 18

THEY CURSED HER BABY

"I bring you a chicken," Barzabai offered the witch doctor. "I need the charm that makes healthy babies."

The witch doctor grinned broadly. He accepted the chicken from Barzabai as she stepped into his dark sitting room. He released the chicken onto the dirt floor, then turned to his bag of charms.

"This will do," he mumbled, selecting a leather wrapped charm. He held the charm high as he began a step-hop dance toward Barzabai, who was sitting on the rug in the middle of the floor. Barzabai watched, wide-eyed, as he lowered the charm and intoned his mantra over it, all the while prancing around Barzabai.

Barzabai did not try to hide her excitement over the coming baby, but the witch doctor's contact with evil spirits frightened her. She would not have come if she had known any other way to be sure of a healthy baby. With a last chant and flourish the witch doctor came to an abrupt stop before her. Bending down, he bound the charm around her neck. Barzabai thanked him and returned to her home, confident the evil spirits were appeased.

A few weeks later Carol's touring team came for their annual week of evangelism in Devthan, Satana District. Bhaurav and Barzabai attended the meetings every evening. Carol taught the village women in the afternoons. Barzabai came faithfully unless she had to work in the field, or gather firewood to sell in a nearby town. She and Bhaurav needed to labor at whatever work they found to meet their daily needs.

Like Lydia in the Bible, Barzabai and Bhaurav soon opened their hearts to believe in the Lord. Suddenly the fear of the evil one was gone. The joy of the Lord shined from their faces. Barzabai took off the charm the witch doctor tied around her neck, for she no longer feared the evil spirits.

Before the week finished they told the missionaries they wanted to be baptized. Carol and the evangelist met with them instructing them about this step of faith. The fact that they were the only ones in Devthan who chose to follow the Lord did not discourage them in the least.

The changes did not go unnoticed by their neighbors. The witch doctor led a group of villagers to confront Barzabai and Bhaurav. One day, as Barzabai went about her work, the witch doctor suddenly blocked her way.

"Where is your charm?" he demanded.

Praying for courage, Barzabai answered, "I threw it away. I believe in Jesus. I no longer fear the evil spirits."

The witch doctor's eyes flashed angrily. "You shall fear," he promised. "Your baby is cursed: it will die."

Barzabai shared her experience with Bhaurav that evening. They prayed together for the baby's safe delivery.

Another day a group of villagers yelled at Barzabai, threatening to cover her with mud and feathers if she and Bhaurav continued to attend classes preparing them for baptism. Again, she and Bhaurav asked the Lord to keep them strong for Him.

A few months later Pastor Sane led the team back to Devthan for the baptismal ceremony at the nearby river. Barzabai and Bhaurav told the missionaries how God kept giving them strength and courage in the face of the angry villagers. The team continued to pray that God would uphold this couple, giving them courage in the time of opposition, and for any test that might follow.

Angry villagers watched the baptism ceremony. They heard Barzabai and Bhaurav's testimony. Their bold witness for the Lord Jesus Christ silenced the dissenters. No one proposed they carry out the plan to cover them with mud and feathers.

When the time came for the birth of Barzabai's baby, as the custom was, she went to her mother's home in another village for the delivery. The labor proceeded normally. They rejoiced in the birth of a healthy baby girl.

Eight days later the baby died. When Carol heard the news, she was tempted to think the Lord had made a mistake. Wouldn't Barzabai and Bhaurav now turn back and deny the Lord?

But God makes no mistakes! Exactly the opposite happened. The next time the team went to Devthan, Barzabai and Bhaurav joyfully took their places with the few believers and declared God was daily strengthening their faith. They listened to God's Word just as eagerly as they had before, anxious to learn God's will so they might continue to grow in grace.

Barzabai missed the baby she had hoped to hold in her arms but God did not forget the longing of her heart. The next year she came to Carol saying, "I think the Lord is going to give us another baby," which upon examination proved to be true.

Her pregnancy continued well until one day Barzabai awoke with a high fever. Her temperature continued to go up and down. After a few days she came to the clinic where Carol determined she had malaria. The treatment at that time was not as effective as it is today. Her temperature dropped for a time each day, followed by a chill. Then it would rise as high as 105 degrees. Carol was very concerned. Quinine was the only antidote, but it might cause her to lose her baby. For several days she and Barzabai prayed about the proper medication, while Barzabai continued to suffer with daily high fevers. Finally Carol decided to give a quinine injection. Barzabai agreed to take it even though she knew of the possible dire consequences. They rejoiced to see God work a miracle: Barzabai not only recovered but the baby suffered no harm.

Barzabai continued to go to the clinic for Carol to check on the baby's progress. One day Carol discovered two different heart beats. Barzabai was carrying twins! Carol arranged for her to stay in a nearby home so she would be close by in case the babies came early or complications developed. The expected time arrived. Carol delivered two beautiful, healthy baby girls. Barzabai and Bhaurav were ecstatic.

"Their names are Naomi and Ruth," Barzabai said. "How wonderful, even though our other baby died, we still have two. How good of the Lord!"

Babies grow quickly. In a few years Ruth and Naomi attended the village school in Devthan and after that the Mission Girls' School in Dharangaon. From 1971 to 1974 the Mission asked Carol to superintend the Girls' School. She had the joy of teaching Bible to Naomi and Ruth while they attended high school there.

From the Mission Girls' School they went to Chinchpada Christian Hospital for nurses training and then to another hospital for further training. In later years they worked with Carol in the Chinchpada hospital.

Through the years the Christian leaders rejoiced to see Barzabai and her children grow in faith. Barzabai never learned to read but her girls read the Bible to her. She faithfully attended women's Bible classes and yearly Bible conferences.

Then came the time for Carol to leave India for the U.S. and for retirement. Barzabai did not forget her. She came to Carol's house, bringing a live chicken. As she sat on Carol's veranda she took the chicken out of a bag and said, "Mai (Big Sister), thank you for telling me about the Lord Jesus and showing me how to be saved. Thank you too for safely bringing my girls, Ruth and Naomi, into this world and for teaching them."

Then she handed Carol the chicken. It was Carol's turn to thank her for the joy of teaching one who allowed the Lord to direct her life.

Bhilwod Bible Class

Chapter 19

BACK TO THE USA

In 1982, because of her health, Carol returned to the United States. She had given 38 years to the Lord, 36 of them in India. She intended to return to her beloved adopted land as soon as her health problems were remedied.

Life in India takes its toll. The life expectancy there is 57 years, even today. Although this is not the expectancy of healthy foreigners, such as Carol, still health deteriorates. This is no surprise to those brave missionaries who give their lives to serve the Lord in so-called "third-world" nations. It is part of the cost that must be considered in the sacrifice.

Carol came home with digestive problems that will dictate to her what she may or may not eat for the rest of her life. She has adjusted well to that and enjoys the spicy Indian food that she first tasted on the train to Amalner. It is a treat to share an authentic Indian meal in Carol's kitchen.

For a few months Carol spent some time in and out of the hospital, this time as a patient. She suffered a great deal of weakness, but she has been gradually regaining her strength.

When she first returned from India, Carol maintained an apartment in Vallejo, provided in part by the Vallejo Bible Church that faithfully undertook her first support. In 1987 she moved to an apartment in San Diego so that she might be closer to her brother, who lives in that area.

The missionary-minded Vallejo Bible Church set aside a special meeting area, known as the Carol Hastings Room. Carol was the first of many missionaries they have supported by prayer and finances over the years.

As her health has returned Carol has gradually added ministries to her life: a Ladies' Bible class while she was in Vallejo and another in her neighborhood in San Diego. She has also attended classes with Indian women, helping them to learn the language and customs they need to manage their business while their husbands attend U. S. universities. She especially enjoys witnessing to several East Indian neighbors.

Another ministry Carol enjoys in San Diego is volunteer work in the library of La Mesa Christian School where Walter Lindquist is administrator. Carol occasionally speaks in their chapel and is available to provide enrichment by relating first-hand facts and experiences from India to classes.

When Carol returned the last time, she faithfully reported to the churches who supported her. This book has been written at the request of several people who heard her story at that time. They felt she should tell

the Christian community what God is doing in the world today and how
God can use a dedicated life.

Carol's dream of returning to India has not yet been realized, but her
heart is still in the land. When she is out shopping or running errands,
Carol is quick to discover Indian people with whom she delights to share
the Gospel.

CURRENT FACTS ABOUT INDIA

TEAM missionaries were nearly the first to enter Satana District and Kalvan of Nasik District, although the earliest TEAM missionaries did hear of a Miss Latham who rode by horseback to some villages in Satana District.

Earlier, possibly during the 1500's, there is evidence that Catholic missionaries from a Portuguese province near the West Coast of India and of Satana District may have ridden horses over the mountains to Kalvan. There were no roads even for bullock carts until very recent times.

History records that Shah Jahan, who built the Taj Mahal as a tomb for his favorite wife, called an ecumenical conference in Agra. He invited representatives from different religions in India, including the Catholics from the Portuguese province. So it is possible that someone representing Christianity might have traveled into the Satana District, but there is no actual historical record of it.

Mrs. Clayton Kent, a TEAM missionary, opened clinics in Satana and Kalvan before Carol arrived. As Indians' physical needs were being met through the medical ministry, villagers became more willing to listen to God's answer for their spiritual needs.

The country of India covers an area 1,269,219 square miles. It is roughly twice the size of the state of Alaska, with a population of 843 million, according to the 1990 census. Its major cities are New Delhi (population 5.2 million) and Bombay (9.9 million).

The government of India is divided into two parts: the executive, consisting of the president, and prime minister and the council of ministers; and the legislative, consisting of the parliament of state and the house of people. There are six major political parties: Congress-I (the largest), Congress-V, All India Dravidian Progressive Federation, Janata Party, and two communist parties.

The population in 1989 exceeded 813 million, with an annual growth rate of 2.24%. 72% are Indo-Aryan, 25% Dravidian, and 2% Mongoloid. India is the second most populous country in the world (after China), having 16% of the world's population. Population density averages 641 persons per square mile.

Religiously, India is 83% Hindu, 11% Muslim, and 3% Christian, or more accurately, "of Christendom."

Indians speak the official language of Hindi, English (particularly for trade), fourteen other main dialects and 1000 minor languages and dialects. Education is compulsory from ages nine to fourteen, and literacy is 52.11%.

Infant mortality is 91 per 1000 births. Life expectancy is 57 years, 25 years of expectancy having been added in the past 20 years.

Indians find employment mainly in agriculture (72%), Manufacturing (9%), government (7%), and tourism (5%).

The India of today is vastly different in many ways from the India Carol entered in 1943. Yet in the important ways it is the same, for men and women still need to hear and believe in the Lord Jesus Christ in order to be saved.